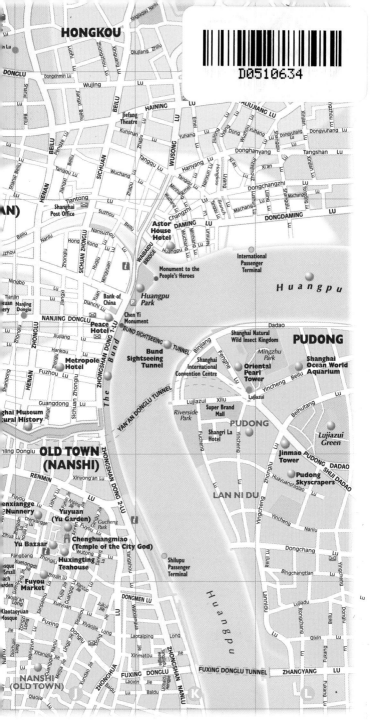

HONGKOU

D0510634

Qiujiang Zhilu

Qiujiang Zhilu

Luchu Lu

Zhongzhou Lu

Xinjiang Lu

Wujing Lu

DONGLU

Dongxinmin Lu

Shanxi Lu

Jiangxi Beilu

HAINING

Kunshan Lu

Jiefang Theatre

Emei Lu

Yuhang Lu

WUSONG

Haimen Lu

Dongbao Lu

Wuhang Lu

Tangshan Lu

SICHUAN

BEILU

HENAN

Tangqu Lu

Wuchang Lu

Hanyang Lu

Tangqu Lu

Liyang Lu

Xi'an Lu

Xinjiang Lu

Dongyuhang Lu

Dongchangzhi Lu

Tangshan Lu

Shanxi Beilu

Fanyu Lu

Tiantong Lu

Tangqu Lu

Changzhi Lu

Minhang Lu

Wusong Lu

Wuchang Lu

Minhang Lu

DAMING LU

Branch Lu

Machangzhi Lu

Shahongkou Lu

DONGDAMING LU

Shanghai Post Office

Astor House Hotel

Huangpu Lu

Wuchang Lu

Minhang Lu

Nansuzhou

International Passenger Terminal

Nanlu

Beilu

Hong Kong Lu

Huqiu Lu

Monument to the People's Heroes

Huangpu Lu

Dianchi Lu

Minyuzhou

Ningbo Lu

Bank of China

Dianchi Lu

H u a n g p u

Tianlin Lu

Nanjing Donglu

NANJING DONGLU

Chen Yi Monument

Huangpu Park

Dadao

Shanghai Natural Wild Insect Kingdom

PUDONG

Jiujiang Lu

Peace Hotel

Bund Sightseeing Tunnel

Binjiang

Fenghe Lu

Mingzhu Park

Shanghai Ocean World Aquarium

Hankou Lu

BUND SIGHTSEEING TUNNEL

Shanghai International Convention Centre

Oriental Pearl Tower

Yincheng Beilu

Metropole Hotel

Fuzhou Lu

HENAN

ZHONGLU

Lujiazui

Lu

Guangdong Lu

Sichuan Zhonglu

YAN'AN DONGLU TUNNEL

The Bund

Lujiazui Xilu

Super Brand Mall

Beihutang

hai Museum ural History

ZHONGSHAN DONG 2-LU

Riverside Park

PUDONG

Yincheng

Lujiazui Green

ning Donglu

OLD TOWN (NANSHI)

RENMIN

Xinyong'an Lu

Fucheng

Shangri La Hotel

Jinmao Tower

PUDONG

DADAO

ZHONGSHAN DONG 2-LU

Fuyou Lu

LU

Lishui Lu

Fumin Anping Lu

Gucheng Park

Yincheng

Huayuanshiqiao

Pudong Skyscrapers

PUDONG SHUI DADAO

enxiangge Nunnery

Chenxiangge

Yuyuan (Yu Garden)

Anren

Fuyou Lu

Zhonghua

LAN NI DU

Yincheng

Lu

Yu Bazaar

Zihua

Chenghuangmiao (Temple of the City God)

Wutong

Nanlu

esque Small ach rden

Fangbang

Kuelongqi

Zhonghua

Huxingting Teahouse

Shouin Lu

Jukui Lie

Dongchang

Lu

Bingchangtian

Lujiadu

Yincheng

Dongju

Lu

Fuyou Market

Fulla Jie

Qixin

Lu

Xiaotaoyuan Mosque

Yaojia'an Long

Xueyuan

Xiaoaolie

Lanmidu

Rongchang

Qixin

Dajing

Wangjia Jie

Jie

Fuxing

Dongjie

Lu

Shilupu Passenger Terminal

H u a n g p u

Xinmatou

Lu

Baochang

Xitangjia Jie

Meijia Jie

Jukui

Lu

Laotaiping

Lu

Long

Dongchang

Yincheng

Lu

NANSHI (OLD TOWN)

J

Qiaolu

ZHONGHUA

Laoxin Jie

FUXING DONGLU

Baidu

Xinmatou Jie

ZHONGSHAN NANLU

K

Yangjia Tidu Lu

FUXING DONGLU TUNNEL

ZHANGYANG

Lanmidu

L

LU

Fukang Lu

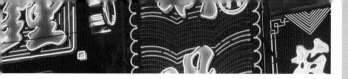

CITYPACK TOP 25
Shanghai

CHRISTOPHER KNOWLES
ADDITIONAL WRITING BY GEORGE MCDONALD

If you have any comments
or suggestions for this guide
you can contact the editor at
Citypack@theAA.com

AA Publishing
Find out more about AA Publishing and the wide
range of services the AA provides by visiting our
website at www.theAA.com/travel

How to Use This Book

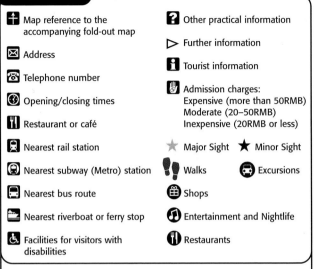

KEY TO SYMBOLS

- ✚ Map reference to the accompanying fold-out map
- ✉ Address
- ☎ Telephone number
- 🕐 Opening/closing times
- 🍴 Restaurant or café
- 🚆 Nearest rail station
- Ⓜ Nearest subway (Metro) station
- 🚌 Nearest bus route
- ⛴ Nearest riverboat or ferry stop
- ♿ Facilities for visitors with disabilities
- ❓ Other practical information
- ▷ Further information
- ℹ Tourist information
- ✋ Admission charges:
  Expensive (more than 50RMB)
  Moderate (20–50RMB)
  Inexpensive (20RMB or less)
- ★ Major Sight   ★ Minor Sight
- 👣 Walks   🚐 Excursions
- 🛍 Shops
- 🎵 Entertainment and Nightlife
- 🍴 Restaurants

This guide is divided into four sections

• Essential Shanghai: An introduction to the city and tips on making the most of your stay.
• Shanghai by Area: We've broken the city into seven areas, and recommended the best sights, shops, entertainment venues, nightlife and restaurants in each one. Suggested walks help you to explore on foot. Farther Afield takes you beyond the center.
• Where to Stay: The best hotels, whether you're looking for luxury, budget or something in between.
• Need to Know: The info you need to make your trip run smoothly, including getting about by public transportation, weather tips, emergency phone numbers and useful websites.

Navigation In the Shanghai by Area chapter, we've given each area its own color, which is also used on the locator maps throughout the book and the map on the inside front cover.

Maps The fold-out map accompanying this book is a comprehensive street plan of Shanghai. The grid on this fold-out map is the same as the grid on the locator maps within the book. We've given grid references within the book for each sight and listing.

HOW TO USE THIS BOOK

Contents

CONTENTS

Introducing Shanghai

Shanghai is one of the fastest-changing cities in the world, seemingly able to transform itself at the drop of a government planning paper or a new commercial proposal, and certainly able to at the drop of a bundle of yuan, yen, dollars or euros.

The Shanghainese themselves would likely tell you that Shanghai is the fastest-changing city in the world, and what's more they're not even properly into their stride.

A combination of vast size, a large and densely packed population, a swirl of fuming traffic, and a here-today-gone-tomorrow approach to just about everything can make this a hard city to get a handle on. Add to this the major problem of air and other pollution, and a populace who are more than a little too busy hustling in order to get and stay ahead to have much time to spare for attending to the social graces, and you have one that can be hard to get close to.

But for many people, both residents and visitors, this hustle and bustle, this energy focused with laser intensity, is all part of the city's character. So long as China's destiny continues to lie with a growing economy and ever-tighter integration into the global community, the road leads through Shanghai, and the Shanghainese know it and are proud of it. As for anyone who doesn't want to be part of China's once-and-future world city, in the same league as New York, London and Tokyo, they can always get out of the way and hang out in laid-back Beijing or Guangzhou.

In the wake of the booming economy, the city is opening its wallet and purse to play hard as well as work hard, and new cultural institutions are helping to round out the city's social life. Shanghai aims to work all the angles but is also working to smooth some of its rough edges. Watching how it is doing all this can be quite an education.

Facts + Figures

- **The population of Shanghai is estimated at around 20 million.**
- **The city generates 5 percent of the nation's annual gross domestic product.**
- **There are some 45,000 taxis in the city.**

HIGH SOCIETY

Around 30 years ago, the Park Hotel, on Nanjing Lu, was the tallest building not just in Shanghai, but in the country. That seems hard to believe now, when the Park Hotel is dwarfed by skyscrapers. Across the Huangpu River, in Pudong, are some of the tallest edifices in the world. Among them is the Oriental Pearl TV Tower, the tallest such tower in Asia.

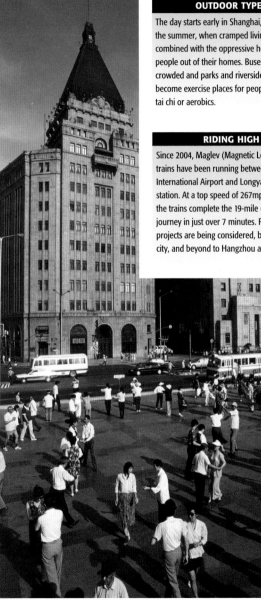

OUTDOOR TYPES

The day starts early in Shanghai, especially in the summer, when cramped living conditions combined with the oppressive heat drive people out of their homes. Buses are soon crowded and parks and riverside areas become exercise places for people practicing tai chi or aerobics.

RIDING HIGH

Since 2004, Maglev (Magnetic Levitation) trains have been running between Pudong International Airport and Longyang Lu metro station. At a top speed of 267mph (430kph), the trains complete the 19-mile (30.5km) journey in just over 7 minutes. Future Maglev projects are being considered, both inside the city, and beyond to Hangzhou and Beijing.

A Short Stay in Shanghai

DAY 1

Morning Start out with breakfast or just coffee at the **Peace Hotel** (▷ 62) to soak up the atmosphere of prewar Shanghai. Walk along the **Bund** (▷ 58) and the waterfront.

Mid-morning Head for **Yuyuan** (Yu Garden; ▷ 74) in the Old Town and relax over a pot of Chinese tea in the **Huxingting Tea House** (▷ 70–71, 79) just outside the garden.

Lunch Have a light and quick lunch (the line of intending diners will likely see to that) lunch of Shanghai steamed dumplings at the grand traditional restaurant **Lu Bo Lang** (▷ 79).

Afternoon Wander the narrow streets of the **Old Town** (▷ 72–73), with their popular dumpling restaurants and antiques and jewelry shops.

Mid-afternoon Stroll through **People's Square** (▷ 38–39) and the neighboring **Renmin Park** (▷ 40). Take in the outstanding bronzes, porcelain and paintings in the **Shanghai Museum** (▷ 42–43).

Dinner Dine on fine Shanghai cuisine at the **Mei Long Zhen** (▷ 51) restaurant on **Nanjing Lu** (▷ 36).

Evening Catch a performance of the superb Shanghai Acrobatic Troupe at the **Shanghai Centre Theatre** (▷ 50) or **Lyceum Theatre** (▷ 30).

DAY 2

Morning Window shop along Nanjing Donglu, the pedestrians-only segment of Nanjing Lu. Have breakfast at the stylish **Park Hotel** (▷ 46) close to People's Square.

Mid-morning In the southwest of the city, see a grandiose piece of old Shanghai in the form of the Catholic Cathedral at **Xujiahui** (▷ 29). By way of contrast, not far from here is the **Longhua Pagoda** (▷ 26), part of a Buddhist temple.

Lunch Have a plain but satisfying lunch at the temple's vegetarian restaurant.

Afternoon Go for a cruise on the **Huangpu River** (▷ 60–61), passing through the port area as far as the confluence with the Yangtze River.

Dinner Cross over the Huangpu to Pudong, and dine at a table with a view in one of the hotel restaurants here—**Jade On 36** (▷ 97) at the Pudong Shangri-La is a good bet, both for the cuisine and the magnificent views.

Evening Pay a second visit to the **Peace Hotel** (▷ 62) to hear its renowned Old Jazz Band.

Top 25

► ► ►

Around Suzhou Creek
▷ **56–57** Former
consulates and grand old
Shanghai mansions.

The Bund ▷ **58–59**
Shanghai's splendid
embankment is lined with
renovated 1920s buildings.

**Duolun Lu Cultural
Street** ▷ **84–85** An
historic street, lined with
restored Shikumen houses.

Yuyuan ▷ **74** The finest
classical garden in Shanghai
and the city's most popular
tourist sight.

Xujiahui Cathedral ▷ **29**
Catholic cathedral easily
recognizable by its twin
spires and redbrick facade.

Xintiandi ▷ **44** A glamorous collection of shops,
entertainment venues and
restaurants in traditional
Shikumen houses.

**Urban Planning
Exhibition Hall** ▷ **37**
Intriguing museum showing
the Shanghai of the future.

Sun Yat-sen's Residence
▷ **28** Sun's European-style
mansion with 1920s interior
preserved intact.

**Soong Qing-Ling's
Residence** ▷ **27** The
home of Sun Yat-sen's
widow, an attractive
European villa and garden.

Shanghai Zoo ▷ **104–105**
Pandas, tigers and other
endangered Chinese species
in an enlightened zoo.

Shanghai Museum
▷ **42–43** World-class
modern museum dedicated
to Chinese arts and crafts.

Shanghai Art Museum
▷ **41** The city's foremost
art gallery displays Chinese
art in the former race club.

These pages are a quick guide to the Top 25, which are described in more detail later. Here they are listed alphabetically, and the tinted background shows which area they are in.

HONGKOU 81-88
Lu Xun Park
ZHABEI
HONGKOU
Duolun Lu Cultural Street
Heping Park
Children's Park
Jiaotong Park

BUND (WAITAN) 53-66
NI CHENG QIAO
Suzhou Creek
Peace Hotel
Huangpu Park
Huangpu
TI LAN QIAO
Renmin Park
Urban Planning Exhibition Hall
People's Square
HUANGPU
The Bund
PUDONG
Oriental Pearl Tower
Riverside Park
Jinmao Tower
Shanghai Museum
Square Park
OLD TOWN (NANSHI) 67-80
Yuyuan (Yu Garden)
LAN NI DU
Lujiazui Green
Pudong Skyscrapers
Huaihai Park
Taipingqiao Park
Xiantiandi Park
Huxingting Teahouse
LUJIAZUI FINANCIAL & TRADE ZONE
LAO XI MEN
LUWAN
NANSHI (OLD TOWN)
PUDONG 89-98

◀ ◀ ◀

Shopping

Shanghai might still have a little way to go before the phrase "shopper's paradise" trips off the lips quite as easily as it does in the case of Hong Kong, Paris and London, but it's getting there, and not so slowly either.

Retail Therapy
Four principal areas have developed as the main hubs of big time shopping in the city. The foremost of these, Nanjing Lu (Nanjing Road; ▷ 36), has long been the main shopping street, not only of Shanghai but of the rest of China as a whole (always excepting Hong Kong, of course, which was returned to China from British rule in 1997). Brand-aware shoppers and designer-label aficionados will likely be at home among such names as Gucci, Cerruti, Yamamoto, Diesel and many others on this long street, which runs west from the Bund and past the northern edge of Renmin Square. Nanjing Lu is no longer the unchallenged colossus, however, and is having to work harder to hold its own. Much of its eastern section, Nanjing Donglu, has been transformed into a pedestrians-only precinct, which has made shopping there a lot more pleasant than it was formerly.

Department Stores
In addition to individual shops and boutiques, Nanjing Lu hosts several of Shanghai's most

NEW AREAS

More major shopping zones are opening up. The most important of these is on the Pudong side of the Huangpu River. Although this area has had a difficult time establishing itself, and some shops have either closed or had to diversify their marketing strategies to cope, it seems that the continual influx of new residents into the area, and the fact that many of the commuters who work here are among the best-paid in the city, is ensuring its future. The New Shanghai Shopping City mall here is a sign of how things are developing.

Traditional shops and markets attract as much attention as chic malls

notable department stores, shopping malls and supermarkets, among them the New World department store (▷ 48), Shanghai Number One department store, the Plaza 66 mall (▷ 48) and the Wellcome Supermarket (▷ 49). Streets running off Nanjing Lu add to its allure with superior shopping malls like Raffles City (▷ 49).

Other Major Streets

Huaihai Lu is Nanjing Lu's fiercest competitor. It doesn't offer much that is different, only more of the same successful formula of shops, boutiques, department stores and malls. As such it appeals mainly to the better-off Chinese and visitors. For those who don't insist on name labels and are looking for something a little or a lot more affordable, the mostly Chinese shops on Sichuan Beilu are popular with ordinary Shanghainese and middle-brow visitors alike. Fuzhou Lu is noted for its culturally oriented shops, selling antiques, old books and fine arts items.

Markets

Shanghai's many street markets are both a resource for reasonably priced goods, and even some bargains, and are an attraction in their own right, filled with local atmosphere. Some of the best are in the Old Town.

Shop for exotic or everyday items in a rapidly growing range of outlets

YUYUAN AREA

Although the rather touristy area in and around the Yu Garden in the Old Town cannot be considered a shopper's paradise in the way that some of the main shopping streets are, in some respects it is more popular with visitors. Here is where they can find no end of antiques, arts and crafts, traditional medicines, souvenirs, and all kinds of minor commodities. Most of these go for reasonable prices—but in most cases only after the purchaser has bargained with great tenacity to achieve this. The crowds that gather here to peruse, bargain and buy are, if anything, more densely packed than those elsewhere.

Shopping by Theme

Whether you're looking for a department store, a quirky boutique, or something in between, you'll find it all in Shanghai. On this page shops are listed by theme. For a more detailed write-up, see the individual listings in Shanghai by Area.

DEPARTMENT STORES AND MALLS

Chia Tai Department Store
  (▷ 97)
Friendship Store (▷ 78)
Hua Lian (▷ 48)
Isetan (▷ 48)
New World (▷ 48)
Plaza 66 (▷ 48)
Raffles City (▷ 49)
Shanghai Spring
  Department Store (▷ 87)
Wal-Mart Supercenter
  (▷ 97)
Westgate Mall (▷ 49)
Yatai Shenghui Shopping
  Centre (▷ 97)

FOOD SHOPS

Carrefour (▷ 87)
City Supermarket (▷ 48)
Jin Jiang Grocery Store
  (▷ 31)
Old Shanghai Teahouse
  (▷ 78)
Parkson Grocery (▷ 48)
Shanghai First Provisions
  Company (▷ 49)
Wellcome Supermarket
  (▷ 49)

MARKETS

Dajing Lu Market (▷ 75)
Dongtai Lu Antiques
  Market (▷ 48)
Fumin Small Commodities
  Market (▷ 78)
Fuyou Market (▷ 76)
Huabao Building Antiques
  Market (▷ 78)
Shanghai Old Street
  (▷ 78)
Shanghai South Bund
  Fabric Market (▷ 78)

SOUVENIRS

China Tourist Souvenir
  Corporation (▷ 48)
Eutoria (▷ 87)
Guo Chun Xiang Curiosity
  Shop (▷ 87)
Shanghai Antique and
  Curio Store (▷ 65)
Shanghai Arts & Crafts
  Service Center (▷ 49)
Shanghai Lyceum Jewelry
  & Antique Store (▷ 31)
Shanghai Museum Shop
  (▷ 49)
Silk Museum (▷ 78)
Yu Bazaar (▷ 76)

TRADITIONAL SHOPS

Caitongde Drugstore
  (▷ 65)
Chinese Ancient Bookstore
  (▷ 65)
Duo Yun Xuan Art Studio
  (▷ 65)
Huangshan Tea Co (▷ 31)
Lao Zhou Hu Cheng
  Chinese Writing Brush
  and Inkstick Store
  (▷ 65)
Lei Yung Shang (▷ 48)
Shanghai Jingdezhen
  Porcelain Artware Store
  (▷ 49)

BEST OF THE REST

Cybermart (▷ 48)
Duty Free Shop (▷ 31)
Garden Books (▷ 31)
Jin Jiang Hotel Bookshop
  (▷ 31)
Shanghai Fashion
  Company (▷ 49)
Shanghai Foreign
  Language Bookstore
  (▷ 49)

Shanghai by Night

Before World War II, Shanghai was notorious for its seedy nightlife, a reputation that brought visitors in search of a good time. That all ended with the postwar Communist takeover. Afterward, as in all of China's cities at the time, nightlife was pretty much conspicuous by its absence.

Traditional to Modern
But Shanghai seemingly never forgot how to have a good time. Now the leading role of the party has taken on an entirely new meaning, as can easily be seen by the way Shanghai lights up after dark. Dance clubs, raves, cocktail bars, pubs and cinemas are all flourishing. And there is an increasing palette of highbrow entertainment to choose from, with offerings both traditional and modern, Chinese and international: classical music, opera, theater, dance, spectacular and artistic acrobatics shows.

Quick Change
It can be hard to keep up with the rapid changes that occur in the nightlife scene. Clubs, pubs and other venues come and go with astonishing ease. Even when an establishment survives, it might up sticks and move to a better location along the same street or to a different part of town. Some nightspots do stand the test of time, but it makes sense to check before getting into a taxi or taking the metro.

LISTINGS

No fewer than four English-language magazines provide visitors and expats with easily accessible what's on information, and three of them have their own websites. The weekly *SH* magazine covers events, listings, reviews and features about the city, what's on where, and more; its associated website (www.8days.sh) keeps you up-to-date online. The monthly magazines *That's Shanghai* and *Shanghai Talk* (www.thatssh.com) do the same, usually in greater depth but the information is not quite so timely. Finally, there's the bi-weekly *City Weekend* magazine's Shanghai edition, online at www.cityweekend.com.cn

...anghai lights up after ...rk with modern pubs, ...bs and cocktail bars and ...ditional Chinese opera

Eating Out

Shanghai is naturally the best place on earth in which to sample Shanghainese cuisine, which connoisseurs consider to be a version of the Huaiyang (also known as Yangzhou) cuisine of the lower Yangtze delta. Chefs working in these styles have, across hundreds if not thousands of years, added to a rich store of dishes, menus, ingredients and cooking methods.

Shanghai Cuisine

The city's indigenous cuisine has a number of distinctive characteristics. The "drunken" label attached to some classic dishes, for instance drunken chicken or drunken crabs, arises because they are either marinated or cooked in alcohol such as rice wine. Vinegar, particularly the famed vinegar produced in nearby Zhejiang, is another popular ingredient. Sugar is often used as a sweetener, though since it is generally combined with vinegar, alcohol or soy sauce—or all three together—it creates a sweet-sour or savory taste. Since the city is so close to the sea, and because it stands on or near to the Huangpu and Yangtze rivers, sea and freshwater fish and crustaceans form a big part of the menu in city restaurants.

International Menus

As befits its status as China's premier international gateway city, Shanghai has indulged itself and its visitors with national cuisine styles from around the world, along with fusion, world, nouvelle and other fancy variations.

CHINESE STYLES

The city is a rapidly growing melting-pot of people from around China. Many have brought their own distinctive regional and even local cuisines with them. There is no shortage of restaurants, ranging from chic high-end places to on-street eateries, serving Cantonese, Sichuan, Pekingese and other major cuisines. You'll also find Tibetan, Mongolian, Xinjiang, Taiwanese, and nowadays even Hong Kong and Maccanese (Macau) restaurants.

There is no shortage of restaurants in Shanghai

Restaurants by Cuisine

There are restaurants to suit all tastes and budgets in Shanghai. On this page they are listed by cuisine. For a more detailed description of each restaurant, see Shanghai by Area.

CANTONESE

Dynasty (▷ 32)
Fu Lin Xuan (▷ 51)
Kam Boat Restaurant
  (▷ 87)

CHINESE (MIXED)

The Gap (▷ 32)
Harn Sheh (▷ 32)
Huxingting Tea House
  (▷ 79)
Mei Long Zhen (▷ 51)
Old Shanghai Tea House
  (▷ 79)
Red Chopsticks (▷ 97)
Shanghai Garden (▷ 66)
Tan Hotpot (▷ 87)
Xiao Shaoxing (▷ 79)

EUROPEAN

Bund 12 (▷ 66)
The Café (▷ 51)
Café de la Seine (▷ 66)
Danieli's (▷ 97)
E-Café (▷ 51)
Fest Brew House (▷ 66)
Jade On 36 (▷ 97)
Mosaic (▷ 66)

INTERNATIONAL

The Atrium Café (▷ 51)
Fifty Hankou Lu (▷ 66)
Hong Dong Korean
  Restaurant (▷ 87)
Judy's Too (▷ 32)
Kathleen's 5 (▷ 51)
Long Bar (▷ 51)
Pucci (▷ 51)
Sasha's (▷ 32)

SHANGHAINESE

1931 Café Pub (▷ 32)
Bao Luo (▷ 32)
The Grape (▷ 32)
Lu Bo Lang (▷ 79)
Magnificent Restaurant
  (▷ 79)
Mao Restaurant (▷ 66)
Nan Xiang (▷ 79)
Shanghai Old Restaurant
  (▷ 79)
Shanghai Restaurant
  (▷ 32)
Whampoa Club (▷ 66)

VEGETARIAN

Gongdelin (▷ 51)
Jade Buddha Temple
  (▷ 51)

If You Like...

However you'd like to spend your time in Shanghai, these top suggestions should help you tailor your ideal visit. Each sight or listing has a fuller write-up in Shanghai by Area.

INTERNATIONAL SHOPPING

Head for Xintiandi (▷ 44) and instantly trendy boutique shopping.
Isetan (▷ 48) offers department-store class, Japanese style.
For Western eatables and other products, visit City Supermarket (▷ 48).
See a veritable melting-pot of international brand names under one roof at New World (▷ 48).

TRADITIONAL SHOPPING

Choose from special Chinese teas and teapots at Huangshan Tea Co (▷ 31).
Shanghai Jingdezhen Porcelain Artware Store (▷ 49) sells fine ceramics from the famed Jingdezhen kilns southwest of Shanghai.
Find antique books and the necessities for doing calligraphy at Chinese Ancient Bookstore (▷ 65).
Shanghai Arts & Crafts Service Center (▷ 49) is the place for genuine souvenirs.

Shopping in Xintiandi (above and top)

LOCAL CUISINE

The Grape (▷ 32) serves Shanghai and Yangzhou cuisine served in a former Orthodox church.
Multiple Chinese cuisine styles are rustled up to memorable effect. Mei Long Zhen (▷ 51).
Dynasty (▷ 32)—not all Shanghainese would agree that Cantonese cuisine is "local," but this is one of the best.
Bao Luo (▷ 32) serves plain but authentic Shanghai food.

Chinese tea (above right); a tasty local dish (right)

The art deco Peace Hotel (below)

CHARACTER HOTELS

Peace Hotel (▷ 62), one of the outstanding colonial-era buildings on the Bund, has upgraded to maintain its cachet into modern times.
Astor House Hotel (▷ 63, 110) dates (through rebuilding) from the early 19th century but has brought its standard decor up-to-date.
Old House Inn (▷ 111) is a small hotel that makes up for for what it lacks in size in old-fashioned class.
Taiyuan Villa (▷ 111), a French renaissance-style villa that's been refitted as an elegant, unpretentious hotel.

HOT AND COOL

New York New York (▷ 65) is a long-running dance club that has moved with the times and kept its cool.
At Bar Rouge (▷ 65) the well-prepared cocktails are followed by well-crafted DJ sounds.
Stay in tune with the latest sounds at Club Absolut (▷ 31) dance club in the French Concession.
Glamour Bar (▷ 65): the name says it all—a glamorous bar, with a great position at the Bund.

Enjoy a cocktail at a smart bar (above) or take in a performance of the Shanghai Acrobatic Troupe in the evening (below)

ENTERTAINING YOURSELF

Cathay Theatre (▷ 31) offers the best Chinese and international cinema in a 1930s art deco gem.

Some of the plays performed at the Shanghai Dramatic Arts Centre (▷ 31) are in English.
Shanghai Conservatory of Music (▷ 31) is a wonderful venue for classical music, both Chinese and Western.
The Lyceum Theatre (▷ 30) is an occasional venue for the highly regarded Shanghai Acrobatic Troupe.

Fuyou Market and Jing'an Temple (below)

LOOKING FOR A BARGAIN

Jin Jiang YMCA Hotel (▷ 109) is a more-than-decent standard hotel aimed at young travelers.

You might just pick up that valuable antique item for a song at Fuyou Market (▷ 76)—but unless you can haggle, don't bank on it.

The vegetarian restaurant in the Jade Buddha Temple (▷ 51) is short on style yet long on taste.

Fumin Small Commodities Market (▷ 78) is one of the places where locals go to secure a bargain.

SCENT OF SANCTITY

Longhua Temple and Pagoda
Shanghai's most venerable Buddhist temple dates back to the Song dynasty. (▷ 26).

Xujiahui Cathedral (▷ 29) was founded by Jesuit priests, and is still a strong-hold of the Chinese Catholic church.

Jing'an Temple (▷ 45), founded during the Ming dynasty, is the proud owner of a great bell.

COLONIAL AIRS AND GRACES

Not everything in the French Concession (▷ 24–25) is French, but enough franco-phone architecture, parks and broad boulevards survives to give the idea of a certain prewar *je ne sais quoi*.

DongHu Hotel (▷ 109) is an art deco mansion that was a haunt of gangsters.

Taiyuan Villa (▷ 111), now a notable hotel, dates from the 1920s.

Soong Qing-Ling's Residence (▷ 27), a 1920s European-style villa, was the home of the the wife of the founder of modern China, Sun Yat-sen.

The popular terrace outside Sasha's Bar (right) and a wall painting (above right) in the French Concession

Shanghai by Area

This area includes colonial architecture and parks, and Xujiahui Cathedral, all complemented by the Longhua Buddhist Temple. In between is a bustling, cosmopolitan district with shops and eateries.

YAN'AN

ZHONGLU

Moller
Villa

Children's
Art Theatre

Fumin

Lu

Julu

Lu

Julu

Lu

NANLU

Jinxian

Lu

Changle

Lu

Changle

Lu

Julu

Lu

Lyceum
Theatre

SHAANXI

Xinle

Maoming

jinjiang
Hotel

Lu

RUIJIN 1 · LU

Changle

Lu

Donghu

Lu

Xiangyang
Park

Okura
Garden
Hotel

Cathay
Theatre

Chengdu

i

Donghu
Hotel

HUAIHAI

Shanxi
Nanlu

ZHONGLU

Astrid
Apartments

St Nicholas
Church

Nanchang

Fuxing
Park

Fenyang

Nanlu

Nanchang

Lu

Gaolan

Sinan

Yandang

Lu

Shanghai
Arts & Crafts
Museum

Fuxing

Zhonglu

FRENCH
CONCESSION

Maoming

Xiangshan

Sun Yat-sen's
Residence

GAOLU

Lu

Ruijin
Building

Fuxing

Zhonglu

Yongkang

Xiangyang

Lu

SHAANXI

NANLU

RUIJIN 2 · LU

Taiyuan
Villa

Yongjia

Lu

Yongjia

Lu

Sinan

Lu

NANBEI

Taojiang

Yongjia

0   500 m

0   500 yds

D   E   F

French Concession and Markets

HIGHLIGHTS

● Fascinating colonial-era architecture
● Excellent shopping
● Fine restaurants and bars
● Theaters and cinemas
● Small but welcome parks

TIP

● Huaihai Zhonglu, which slices laterally through the French Concession, runs for 3.5 miles (6km). Three Metro stations–Huangpi Nanlu, Shaanxi Nanlu and Changpu Lu–are dotted along it.

In the old days, if you wanted a bohemian lifestyle and to taste the high life, you left the International Concession and its Anglo-American obsession with commerce, and crossed over to "Frenchtown."

France Outre Mer The French Concession lay to the south of the original British Settlement, and to the west of the old Chinese town. Having grown to an area of 4sq miles (10sq km), it refused the invitation to join the Americans and British in forming the International Settlement in 1863. The French Settlement had its own buses and trams, its own electricity and its own judicial system and traffic regulations—and it added spice to the steaming cosmopolitan brew that was Shanghai. Gangsters and revolutionaries, bon-vivants and refugees were attracted to the Concession and by

Clockwise from the left: Pedestrians on busy Huaihai Zhonglu; a reading outlet; examining the items on a clothing stall at Xiang Yang market; the traffic passing along Huaihai Zhonglu; Xiang Yang market; inside Old China Hand Reading Room

1930 French residents were easily outnumbered by Americans, Britons and Russians.

Touring the French Concession The heart of the old concession was Avenue Joffre, today's Huaihai Zhonglu, which is still at least as good a shopping street as the more famous Nanjing Lu (▷ 36). Along here are a few reminders of the past— bakers selling European-style confections and the old Red House Restaurant, formerly Chez Louis, once famous for its soufflé Grand Marnier. Fuxing Park (▷ 30), laid out in the Parisian style with wide paths flanked by trees, is very pretty. The Jin Jiang Tower (▷ 112), built in 1931 as a private hotel for French residents, is where the Shanghai Communiqué was signed in 1972. Opposite is the grandiose entrance to the former French club, Le Cercle Sportif Français, built before World War II.

THE BASICS

➕ C7–F7
✉ Around Huaihai Zhonglu
🍴 Many excellent restaurants
🚇 Shaanxi Nanlu
🚌 10, 42, 911
♿ None

Longhua Temple and Pagoda

The gates to the temple; worshippers inside; a carved lion

THE BASICS

- Off map at A9
- 2853 Longhua Lu
- 6456 6085
- Daily 8–4
- Excellent vegetarian restaurant on premises
- 41, 44, 73, 104, 864
- None
- Inexpensive

HIGHLIGHTS

- Handsome pagoda
- Active temple

TIP

- The best times to visit the temple are at New Year or during one of the festivals: Birthday of the Queen of Heaven (Mar 23), Birthday of Sakyamuni Buddha (Apr 8), Temple Fair (May Day Holiday Week and October National Vacation Week). There are processions and traditional music.

"The ancient temple stands tall and proud, The pagoda towers into the cloud. Willows encircle the river village, Streams are reddened by the blooming peach".
From a Tang dynasty poem.

The pagoda This pagoda's survival is akin to a miracle—something that smacked so obviously of "old China" should have been a prime target during the Cultural Revolution. The foundations of the pagoda date from AD977 (Song dynasty) and although it has doubtless been rebuilt many times since then, it retains the architectural features of the Song period. Seven floors and 134 feet (41m) high, it is octagonal and made of wood and brick, with "flying" eaves of gray tile. It stands on the site of another pagoda thought to have been built during the period known as the Three Kingdoms (AD238–251).

The temple According to legend, the Longhua Temple was founded during the Three Kingdoms period by the king of Wu and Kang Monk Hui, the son of an eminent minister, who was attracted by this marshy area where "the water and the sky were of one color." It is more likely that its earliest construction was during the Five Dynasties period (AD923–979). In any event, the current buildings date from the end of the 19th century, during the final (Qing) dynasty. After years of neglect the temple reopened and there are several dozen monks in residence. The temple and its surroundings are noted for their spring peach blossom.

The garden; a limousine presented to Soong Qing-Ling

Soong Qing-Ling's Residence

宋慶齡
1893-1981

08-01405

Come here to see how the wealthy lived in old Shanghai and to reflect on a vital period in China's modern history. Its former owner, Soong Qing-Ling, remained something of a revolutionary icon despite her family background.

Soong Qing-Ling Born in Shanghai in 1893 to a family whose business was bible printing, Soong Qing-Ling was introduced to Sun Yat-sen through her father's connections with secret societies dedicated to the fall of the emperor. In 1913, on her way home from the US, where she was educated, she met Sun in Japan rallying support for the restoration of the republic he had founded in 1911. She became his secretary and married him in 1915. After Sun's death she became disenchanted with his successor Chiang Kai Shek and went to Moscow, returning to help with the anti-Japanese war effort. After the revolution she held a number of government posts and became a useful symbol for China until her death in 1981.

The residence Soong Qing-Ling's home in Shanghai from 1948 to 1963, in the heart of the French Concession, dates from the 1920s. The house, a European-style villa with a pretty garden, has been maintained as it was on the day that she died. As befits the home of a representative of the people, it is furnished fairly simply, although there is an interesting collection of gifts received from a number of eminent visitors, including a carpet from Mao, and a work in bamboo from Kim Il Sung of North Korea.

THE BASICS

www.shsoong-chingling.com
+ B8
✉ 1843 Huaihai Zhonghlu
🕐 Daily 9–11 and 1–4.30
☎ 6474 7183
🚍 10, 42, 911
♿ None
💰 Inexpensive

HIGHLIGHTS

● Interesting prewar villa and garden
● Insight into the personality cult

Sun Yat-sen's Residence

Exterior view; a portrait on the walls of the cool interior

THE BASICS

🔢 F7
✉ 7 Xiangshan Lu
☎ 6437 2954
🕐 Daily 9–4.30
🚇 Shaanxi Nanlu
🚌 2, 17, 24, 36, 42
✋ Inexpensive

HIGHLIGHT

● Handsome period villa furnished as it was when lived in by Dr. Sun Yat-sen

This small house in the French Concession is a reminder that Dr. Sun Yat-sen was the moving force behind the creation of a Chinese republic early in the 20th century. He lived here until his death in 1925.

Sun the revolutionary Sun Yat-sen was born close to Canton in 1866. He grew up as China tottered under the corrupt anachronism that was the Qing government and, although he was trained as a doctor, his real interest was in political reform. Sun founded the "Revive China Society," which marked the beginning of serious republican agitation. Forced to flee abroad, he was kidnapped by the Qing authorities in London and held in the Chinese Legation. Intervention from the British Foreign Office led to his release. But it was not until 1911 that his alliances with secret societies and elements in the Qing army bore fruit, as disturbances throughout China culminated in rebellion in Wuhan and the final overthrow of the last dynasty, when Sun became president.

The residence Sun came to live in Shanghai in 1920 with his wife Soong Qing-Ling. Xiangshan Lu, in the French Concession, was then Rue Molière. In this small house with an arcaded portico and a garden, Sun was courted by emissaries of the Soviet Union, who were anxious to spread their brand of revolution to China. The house is supposedly as it was during his life, simply furnished in a mixture of Western and Chinese styles, with additional photographs and mementoes of the period.

The cathedral's ornate ceiling (below) and altar (right)

Xujiahui Cathedral

In a country of Buddhist, Confucian and Taoist traditions that is now officially atheist, perhaps nothing is more surprising than the twin towers of a redbrick neo-Gothic cathedral poking into the sky in the shadow of gleaming skyscrapers.

The Jesuits The influence of Jesuit missionaries was felt in Shanghai from as early as the 16th century. An early convert was one Xu Guangqi, a native of Xujiahui, or "Xu Family Village," which at that time was well outside the original town of Shanghai. Xu, an official in the Imperial library, was baptized Paul. He later bequeathed family land to the Jesuits where an observatory and cathedral would eventually be constructed. Following persecution of the converts, the first church here became a temple to the god of war; after the Treaty of Nanking (1842), the land was given to the French, and in 1848 a Jesuit settlement was firmly established.

The cathedral The current cathedral of St. Ignatius was built in 1906 with two 165-foot (50m) spires and capacity for a congregation of 2,500. The interior includes a number of decorative idiosyncracies that indicate Buddhist influence—melons appear on the nave columns and, along with stylized bats (a Chinese symbol of happiness), in the windows. Outside, gargoyles fringe the roof and a holy grotto has been built in the garden. Severely damaged during the Cultural Revolution, the cathedral is now a busy place of worship.

THE BASICS

✚ A9
✉ 158 Puxi Lu
☎ 6469 0930
🕐 Daily
🚇 Xujiahui
🚌 3, 42, 50
♿ None
💵 Free
❓ Services Mon–Fri 6am, 7am; Sat 6am, 7am, 6pm; Sun 6am, 8am

HIGHLIGHTS

● European neo-Gothic among the skyscrapers
● Idiosyncratic detail

TIP

● Be sure to view the new stained-glass windows, Chinese-theme replacements for images destroyed during the Cultural Revolution.

More to See

DONGHU HOTEL
One of the villas (No. 7) that comprise this art deco hotel once belonged to the infamous prewar gangster, Du Yuesheng (▷ 124).
✚ D7 ✉ 70 Donghu Lu ☎ 6415 8158 ⊙ Daily ⦿ Restaurants ⊜ Shaanxi Nanlu ⊟ 44, 49 ⚠ None ⚜ Free

FUXING PARK
Fuxing Park was a private garden, which, in 1908, was turned into a park in the Parisian style, with wide walkways bounded by trees. It is a pleasant and tranquil spot for a stroll.
✚ F7 ✉ Fuxing Zhonglu ⊙ Daily ⦿ Restaurants ⊜ Huangpi Nanlu ⊟ 24 ⚠ None ⚜ Free

LYCEUM THEATRE
This prewar theater where many of the world-famous stars of the era performed is now a multipurpose venue and occasionally hosts the Shanghai Acrobatic Troupe.
✚ E6 ✉ 57 Maoming Nanlu ☎ 6279 8663 ⊟ 42, 48

MOLLER VILLA
A classic piece of Shanghai architecture; a curious concoction of Gothic towers and spires that looks as if it might suit Count Dracula. It was the home of a Scandinavian shipping magnate. Now restored and opened as a hotel, it can be freely visited.
✚ E6 ✉ 30 Shaanxi Nanlu ☎ 6247 8881 ☎ Shaanxi Nanlu ⊟ 42

SHANGHAI ARTS & CRAFTS MUSEUM
This museum of traditional Chinese arts and crafts, is in an elegant mansion with a beautiful garden.
✚ D8 ✉ 79 Fenyang Lu ☎ 6437 3454 ⊙ Daily 8.30–4.30 ⊜ Changshu Lu ⊟ 42 ⚠ None ⚜ Inexpensive

TAIYUAN VILLA
A splendid French Concession mansion built in 1920. It is now a small hotel (▷ 111).
✚ D8 ✉ 160 Taiyuan Lu 2–68 ⊜ Hengshan Lu ⊟ 42 ⚠ None ⚜ Free

A program board outside the Lyceum Theatre (left) and a wider view of the exterior (below)

Shopping

DUTY FREE SHOP
Store in the grounds of Shanghai Stadium.
✚ Off map at A10 ✉ 666 Tianyaoqiao Lu ☎ 6426 6988 Ⓜ Shanghai Stadium

GARDEN BOOKS
This is an airy bookstore selling books on a wide range of subjects. There are also international magazines for sale.
✚ G7 ✉ 325 Changle Lu ☎ 5404 8728 Ⓜ Shaanxi Nanlu

HUANGSHAN TEA CO
Everything required for tea including ceramics and Yixing teapots.
✚ F7 ✉ 605 Huaihai Zhonglu ☎ 5306 2258 Ⓜ Huangpi Nanlu 🚌 42, 911

JIN JIANG GROCERY STORE
Western and Chinese groceries with bakery, stationery and toiletries.
✚ G7 ✉ 175 Changle Lu ☎ 6258 2582 ext. 9603 🚌 126

JIN JIANG HOTEL BOOKSHOP
This good bookshop is within the precincts of the old Jin Jiang Tower.
✚ G7 ✉ 59 Maoming Nanlu ☎ 6472 1273 🚌 126

SHANGHAI LYCEUM JEWELRY & ANTIQUES STORE
Antiques, jewelry, paintings, porcelain, seals.
✚ E6 ✉ 398 Changle Lu ☎ 6255 1667 Ⓜ Shaanxi Nanlu 🚌 42, 48

Entertainment and Nightlife

CAMERA LA
Pleasant place for a quiet drink and a snack, with two rooms, one a bar, the other a café. The decor is stucco and art prints.
✚ D7 ✉ 359 Xinhua Lu ☎ 6280 1256 🕐 2pm–2am 🚌 48

CATHAY THEATRE
A restored treasure of 1930s art deco, the cinema has three screens that show Chinese and new international films.
✚ E7 ✉ 870 Huaihai Zhonglu ☎ 5404 0415/5404 2095 Ⓜ Shaanxi Nanlu 🚌 41

CHARLIE'S
One of the best hotel bars in the city, this intimate, dark and lively bar is justly popular.
✚ A7 ✉ Crowne Plaza Hotel, 400 Panyu Lu ☎ 6145 8888 🕐 2pm–2am 🚌 76

CLUB ABSOLUT
Known for its up-to-the-minute dance music, this is one of the most fashionable places in Shanghai.
✚ G7 ✉ 122 Shanxi Nanlu ☎ 6279 4999 🕐 9.30pm–2.30am 🚌 42

COTTON CLUB
Nice little American-style bar—videos and pictures of US movie stars lend atmosphere—live rock music most evenings.
✚ C7 ✉ 8 Fuxing Xilu ☎ 6437 7110 🕐 8pm–3.30am Ⓜ Changshu Lu 🚌 96

SHANGHAI CONSERVATORY OF MUSIC
Regular performances of classical Chinese and Western music most Sunday evenings.
✚ F7 ✉ 20 Fenyang Lu ☎ 6437 0137 ext. 2166 🚌 96

SHANGHAI DRAMATIC ARTS CENTRE
The center's three modern theaters are as dramatic as the performances of modern and traditional Chinese and Western plays—some of the latter in English—that are put on here.
✚ B7 ✉ 288 Anfu Lu ☎ 6431 6775 Ⓜ Changshu Lu 🚌 49

Restaurants

PRICES

Prices are approximate,
based on a 3-course
meal for one person.

$$$ more than 250RMB
$$ 100–250RMB
$ under 100RMB

1931 CAFÉ PUB ($–$$)

Good Shanghai snacks
(beef soup noodles,
seafood congee) and
dishes from other parts
of China are served in a
small area in a relaxed
way. Old Shanghai prints
line the walls.
🞖 E6 ✉ 112 Maoming
Nanlu ☎ 6472 5264
🕐 Daily 11am–1am
🚇 24

BAO LUO ($)

Easy to miss but hard to
forget, this plain but
inviting restaurant serves
uncompromisingly
traditional Shanghainese
cuisine, which is just
what the many locals
who pile in here, and the
visitors who join them,
have come to enjoy.
🞖 D5 ✉ 271 Fumin Lu
🕐 5403 7239 🚇 Daily
11–6 🚇 Changshu Lu

DYNASTY ($$$)

The sort of plush
Chinese restaurant
usually found in Hong
Kong, this hotel dining
room offers creative
Cantonese-style cooking,
including lobster sashimi
and pork in lotus leaf.
🞖 Off map at A6

✉ Renaissance Yangzi Jiang
Hotel, 2099 Yan'an Xilu
☎ 6275 0000 🕐 Lunch,
dinner 🚇 57

THE GAP ($$–$$$)

This quirky restaurant is
close to the Jin Jiang
Tower and has an old
car clinging precariously
above the entrance. The
atmosphere inside is
southern European,
with wood panels and
plants. The food is
mixed in style, with an
emphasis on north
Chinese cooking.
🞖 E6 ✉ 127 Maoming
Nanlu ☎ 6433 9028
🕐 Daily 11am–midnight
🚇 Shaanxi Nanlu 🚇 126

THE GRAPE ($$)

In a former church, the
service is friendly and
the Shanghai and
Yangzhou cooking, reli-
able. Try the Yangzhou
fried rice, the salt-and-
pepper pork chops and
the claypot eggplant
with vermicelli.
🞖 D6 ✉ 55 Xinle Lu
☎ 5404 0486 🕐 Lunch,
dinner 🚇 45

EXPENSIVE OPTIONS

Always check the cost of
dishes that do not have a
price on them on the
menu. Seasonal dishes,
particularly those involving
seafoods, can be expensive,
even on an otherwise
inexpensive menu.

HARN SHEH ($)

Taiwanese snacks and
fruit teas, including cold
papaya tea and taro ball
milk tea at this teahouse.
🞖 C7 ✉ 10 Hengshan Lu
☎ 6474 6547 🕐 Daily
10am–11pm 🚇 Changshu Lu

JUDY'S TOO ($$)

Modern, comfortable
and spacious bar and
restaurant that's at once
Western and Chinese.
There is also a terrace.
Dishes include pastas,
steaks, soups and salads.
🞖 E7 ✉ 176 Maoming
Nanlu ☎ 6473 1417
🕐 Daily 6pm–midnight
🚇 Shaanxi Nanlu 🚇 96

SASHA'S ($–$$)

A rambling, rose-hued
1920s villa is the setting
for this cool restaurant
and bar. There's elegant
international dining in an
upstairs room, and casual
munching on pizzas and
sundry snacks in the bar
or on the garden terrace.
🞖 C7 ✉ 11 Dongping Lu
☎ 6474 6628 🕐 Daily
11.30–2, 5.30–10
🚇 Changshu Lu

SHANGHAI RESTAURANT ($$–$$$)

A wide range of local
delicacies including
Dazha crab and stir-fried
eels are served in the
bright, modern surround-
ings of the Jianguo Hotel.
🞖 A8 ✉ 439 Caoxi Beilu
☎ 6439 9299 🕐 Lunch,
dinner 🚇 Xiujiahui 🚇 42,
43, 50

The frenetic Nanjing Lu shopping street skirts the edge of Shanghai's concentration of governmental and cultural installations around the People's Park and Square.

Nanjing Lu

The bright lights and busy traffic reflect the popularity of this road

THE BASICS

➕ C6–J5
🍴 Many excellent restaurants
🚇 Nanjing Donglu, People's Park, West Nanjing Road, Jing'an Si
🚌 5, 20, 37
♿ None

HIGHLIGHTS

● Heart of workaday Shanghai
● Excellent shopping
● Period architecture

TIP

● Although much of Nanjing Lu is a veritable cataract of noise and traffic at the best of times, relief can be had in the stretch between Xizang Zhonglu at People's Park in the west and Henan Zhonglu, three blocks from the Bund, in the east. This is the traffic-free (except at intersections) Nanjing Lu Pedestrian Mall, which dates from 1999.

Mention Shanghai to a Chinese person and the chances are that they will think of Nanjing Lu, the Nanjing Road. It has always represented the height of style and the best of shopping in China.

The past The name of Shanghai's most famous thoroughfare commemorates the treaty of the same name which, in 1842, gave trading rights to the foreign powers of the era. As Shanghai grew, so did Nanjing Lu, snaking through the heart of the International Settlement to become, at its western end, the Bubbling Well Road (Nanjing Xilu), named after a well near the Jing'an Temple.

Today Although now rivaled by Huaihai Lu for shopping, Nanjing Lu remains the city's pre-eminent thoroughfare, with the Bund and the Huangpu River at its eastern end. Nanjing Donglu (Nanjing Road East), the most lively section, begins at the Peace Hotel and passes many shops, some dating from pre-World War II, others startlingly modern additions. Some, like the smaller food shops, and the calligraphy shop and arts and crafts café at 422 are of interest because of their traditional goods; others, like the department stores near the intersection with Xizang Lu, are the new incarnations of old prewar department stores. Where Nanjing Donglu meets Nanjing Xilu (Nanjing Road West) is the old racecourse grandstand and clock, now the home of the Shanghai Art Museum (▷ 41), and the Park Hotel, the tallest building outside the Americas at the time of its construction in 1934.

Exterior of the hall (below); scale models of the city (right)

Urban Planning Exhibition Hall

This fascinating museum (Chengshi Guihua Zhangshiguan), on the eastern end of People's Square propels visitors into the future by showing them what the city might look like in the year 2020.

What's in a name? They could easily have given this museum a more attractive name, but don't judge it on this basis alone. Begin your odyssey on the mezzanine floor, where a 20-minute film takes you on a whistle-stop tour of 100 years of Shanghai history.

City plans Prepare to be bowled over by the star attraction, a scale model of the city as it is planned to look in the year 2020, so detailed that it takes up the entire third floor. The high-tech displays on the fourth floor turn the spotlight on mammoth construction projects like the Yangshan deep-water port and the Shanghai World Expo site.

Relentless change One rather sad exhibit is of those older areas that are slated for demolition only to be replaced by soulless modern apartments and office towers. Not all of this will be considered a loss by their current residents, whose wish for more comfortable accommodations will be fulfilled. Yet parts of town that might well be worth saving and refurbishing will disappear, too, and there seems to be nothing to stop the development juggernaut that has already rolled over so many parts of old Shanghai. In partial compensation, there are working re-creations of old shops and teahouses in the museum basement.

THE BASICS

www.supec.org

🔲 G6

✉ 100 Renmin Dadao

☎ 6372 2077

🕐 Mon–Thu 9–6, Fri 9–6 (last ticket one hour before closing)

🍴 Museum café

🚇 People's Square

🚌 40, 71, 123, 574

♿ Moderate

⟁ Few

HIGHLIGHTS

● Scale model of Shanghai's 2020 vision
● Public transportation exhibits on how easy it will one day be to get around Shanghai (but not yet!)
● Top-floor café

TIP

● Take an opera glass or a small pair of binoculars for close-up views of the beautifully detailed scale model of Shanghai in 2020.

People's Square

HIGHLIGHTS
● Shanghai Museum
● Renmin Park
● Grand Theatre
● Shanghai Art Museum

TIP
● There are fine views of the square from the glassed-in terrace of Kathleen's 5 restaurant (▷ 51) on the fifth floor of the Art Museum, and the fifth-floor viewing gallery of the Urban Planning Exhibition Hall.

This unashamedly modern square is the bustling heart of Shanghai. The attractions here include three excellent museums, the Grand Theatre and Renmin Park (▷ 40).

History The British built the largest racecourse in the Far East here in 1862. Meetings were held twice a year and were such important events on the Shanghai calendar that foreign banks and businesses closed early. When the Japanese occupied the city in 1941 they turned the race track into an internment camp for enemy nationals. The square was redesigned in the 1990s.

Seeing the sights The best way to negotiate People's Square (Renmin Guangchang) is to take the metro exit to Renmin Dadao (People's

Clockwise from left: A small child feeds the pigeons; early-morning workers cross the square; outdoor exercises; kite-flying is a popular pastime; the top floors of the Radisson Hotel on the square

Avenue), which divides the square in half. All places of interest, with the exception of the Shanghai Museum (▷ 42) and the Museum of Contemporary Arts (MOCA), are on the north side. Following the avenue east to west will bring you to the main entrance of the Urban Planning Exhibition Hall (▷ 37). Continue past the city hall and the next main building is the Grand Theatre (▷ 45). Turn right out of the avenue and you will see the clock tower of the art museum (▷ 41) and (just beyond) the entrance to Renmin Park. People's Square seems ideally designed to host the mass adulatory parades so beloved by an earlier generation of Communist Party leaders, so it is refreshing to note that the Shanghainese themselves fill it with their own brand of relaxation, and that ballroom dancing, flying kites and feeding the pigeons takes precedence over formal state rituals.

THE BASICS

➕ G6
✉ People's Square
🍴 Restaurants and cafés
Ⓜ People's Square
🚌 46, 71, 123, 574
♿ Good

Renmin Park

TOP 25

Flowers and trees make a pleasant environment in the center

HIGHLIGHTS

● Small lake
● Trees provide welcome shade in summer
● People-watching

TIP

● Greet the dawn in the park with the many people who start the day with a tai chi session.

The People's Park, opposite the Park Hotel, has been created out of what was once the racecourse. It provides a pleasant area to enjoy the fresh air away from the crowds and shops on Nanjing Lu.

Park life Many visitors overlook the pleasant, tranquil green space of Renmin Park. There are flowerbeds and manicured lawns, a Chinese garden, a rock formation, a lotus pond and a pavilion with a Moroccan-style terrace bar and restaurant. The park is popular with office workers at lunchtime and in summer any tree-shaded park bench is much in demand. If you have young children in tow, head for the play area, or look out for pigeons and doves to feed.

Gentle pursuits The racecourse had existed from 1862 and drew gamblers from around China, but did not long survive the Communist takeover in 1949. In those parts of the park with narrow paths and fairly dense assemblages of trees and plants organized into a rigorously formal, landscaped setting, the tai chi practitioners, stylized sword-fighters and kite flyers are not so much to be seen—they are more likely to be found in the open spaces and on the adjoining People's Square (▷ 38). Groups of retired Chinese play mahjongg and chess, brush up on their ballroom dancing and English (native speakers out for a stroll are popular "victims" for the latter), and engage in matchmaking plays for their grandchildren who are far too busy climbing the corporate ladder and having fun to find time for mere matrimony.

Clock tower (below) and sculptures (right) outside the museum

⭐ Shanghai Art Museum

The museum (Shanghai Meishuguan), which opened in 1996, occupies the former premises of the racecourse club, built by the British in 1933. This collection of Chinese art is unmissable.

A bonus The building is worth seeing in its own right for its graceful original clock tower, and because many original art deco features have survived, including the horse's head motifs on the balustrades, the original marble floors and wooden panels, even a brick fireplace or two.

Exhibitions On the museum's five floors are 12 exhibition rooms (and the chic Kathleen's 5 restaurant on the top floor, ▷ 51), which cover Chinese paintings, ink-wash sketches, calligraphy and craft movements and periods from ancient to modern times. Not only Chinese art is accorded respect, and both classic and cutting-edge visiting international art exhibitions have already become something of a tradition (one exhibition was devoted to the fashion of Giorgio Armani).

The collection The museum's collection of modern Chinese art ranges from oil paintings and pop art to calligraphy and traditional Chinese painting. Frustratingly there is little in the way of English translation, so the best times to visit are during the Shanghai Biennale or when the museum hosts exhibitions by both Chinese and international artists. Visitors can sign up for classes in traditional Chinese painting and sketching; and there are lectures, most but not all of which are in Chinese.

THE BASICS

www.sh-artmuseum.org.cn
(in Chinese only)
➕ G6
✉ 325 Nanjing Xilu
☎ 6327 2829
🕐 Daily 9–5; Biennale Oct–Nov, even years
🍴 Kathleen's 5 (▷ 51)
Ⓟ People's Square
🚌 46, 71, 123, 574
♿ Few
💲 Inexpensive

HIGHLIGHTS

● Clock tower of the old racecourse grandstand
● Temporary and visiting exhibitions
● Exhibitions at the Shanghai Biennale
● Kathleen's 5 restaurant (▷ 51) on the 5th floor

Shanghai Museum

One of the great museums of the world, it houses an unparalleled collection of bronzes, porcelain and scroll paintings. Even if you do not care for museums, this is one that should not be missed.

The new museum The original Shanghai Museum was established in 1952 in the old Horse Racing Club on Nanjing Lu. In 1959 it was moved to Henan Lu and located in the former Zhong Hui Bank, once owned by the powerful gangster Big-eared Du (▷ 124). In 1996 a new museum on People's Square, built especially to contain the collection of some 120,000 cultural relics, was opened to the public in 11 galleries and three exhibition halls. From the outside it is the unique architectural style that catches the eye with a design consisting of a square base and a

Clockwise from left: The imposing entrance to the museum; Yi water vessel from 771BC; stone lions guarding the courtyard; Qin dynasty (17th–20th century) woman's embroidered velvet jacket; a wider view showing the circular upper level; a painting of a woman with a sword

circular crown from which emanate four archlike handles—the ensemble is supposed to represent a Han dynasty bronze mirror on an ancient bronze ding tripod (a food container).

Exhibits The theme layout and the lighting organizes and displays the exhibits to their best advantage. Although there are a number of different themes, the three principal exhibitions are those of bronzes and stone sculpture on the ground floor, ceramics on the first floor, and paintings on the second floor. Some of the noble bronze vessels, dating from as far back as the 3rd century AD, are particularly fine, as are the delicate Celadon ceramic wares. Other galleries display jade, Chinese coins, seals, calligraphy, traditional furniture and the art of China's minority peoples. There are also cafeterias and two excellent shops.

THE BASICS

www.shanghaimuseum. net

🚩 G6

✉ 201 People's Square

☎ 6372 3500

🕐 Daily 9–5

🍴 Good cafés on the premises

🚇 People's Square

🚌 46, 71, 123, 574

♿ Few

💰 Moderate

❓ Audio tours, high definition Graphics Hall

Xintiandi

Shikumen House Museum (left); a side street in the area (below)

THE BASICS

⊞ G7
⊠ Huangpi Nanlu
☎ 6311 2288
🍴 Many options
Ⓜ Huangpi Nanlu
🚌 13, 42, 63, 109
♿ Good
ℹ Opposite Shikumen Museum   ⏰ Daily 10–10

HIGHLIGHTS

● Shikumen (stone-frame) houses
● Taipingqiao Park
● Trendy restaurants and cafés
● Boutique stores

TIP

● Xintiandi is just the first part of a redevelopment project of the zone around Taipingqiao Park. It is interesting to peruse the district to see how the changes are progressing. Be sure to take time out for a stroll around the handsome park, which has a pond at its heart.

Akin to a Shikumen theme park, the popular shopping and entertainment complex of Xintiandi opened in 2001. It is a highly successful mix of cafés, stylish restaurants, boutiques, galleries, business premises and an excellent museum.

Housing project Shanghai's distinctive Shikumen houses developed in the 19th century, a fusion of Chinese and Western building styles. By the early 1900s styles had changed and they started falling into disrepair. In the 1990s developers hit on the idea of preserving the unique architecture of one run-down 1930s Shikumen area by changing the buildings' function from residential to shops and restaurants—while preserving the antique exteriors' walls and tiles.

Private history The history of the area and the cultural significance of the buildings are explained in the superb Shikumen House Museum, which also presents a detailed picture of the daily life of a typical family living here in the 1930s. The rooms are crammed with everyday objects and personal effects—movie posters, typewriters, radios, scent bottles, toys. The *tingzijia* or "staircase room" between the first and second floors was usually rented out because its north-facing aspect made it cold in winter and stiflingly hot in summer. The pithily named Memorial House of the First National Congress of the Communist Party of China speaks for itself. The main exhibit is a waxwork diorama dramatizing the founding congress of the Chinese Communist Party.

More to See

GRAND THEATRE
China's first purpose-built opera house was designed by French architect Jean-Marie Charpentier and opened to the public in 1998. The main stage is the largest in the world. The theater is open for tours on Monday mornings.

➕ G6 ✉ 300 Renmin Dadao ☎ 6386 8686/6372 8701 🕐 Guided tours Mon 9–11; box office daily 9–7.30 🚇 People's Square 🚌 46, 71, 123, 574 ♿ Moderate 🖐 Guided tours inexpensive

JING'AN SI (JING'AN TEMPLE)
The western part of Nanjing Lu was known as Bubbling Well Road until 1949. Before that it was Jing'an Road, named after this temple (the Temple of Tranquillity), which has stood on the site for over 1,700 years. The current buildings, which date from the Ming (1368– 1644) and Qing (1644–1912) dynasties, were restored in 1984 and there are over 50 Buddhist monks residing here.

➕ C5 ✉ 1686 Nanjing Xilu 🕐 Daily

🚇 Jingan Si 🚌 20, 37 ♿ None 🖐 Inexpensive

SHANGHAI CENTRE
www.shanghaicentre.com
This complex was an early (1990) indicator of the the way Shanghai was heading. It incorporates luxury apartments, a shopping mall, dining and entertainment venues, the Shanghai Centre Theatre (▷ 50) and the Portman Ritz-Carlton Shanghai hotel.

➕ D5 ✉ 1376 Nanjing Xilu ☎ 6279 8600 🚇 Jing'an Si

SHANGHAI EXHIBITION CENTRE
The gargantuan center is a legacy of the period during the 1950s when the Soviet Union was allied to China. It is a confection in the grandiose style that was the hallmark of Soviet architecture. Mainly used today for trade exhibitions, the building also houses a gigantic arts and crafts shop.

➕ D6 ✉ 1000 Yan'an Zhonglu 🕐 Daily 🍴 Excellent restaurant 🚇 Jing'an Si 🚌 49, 71 ♿ None 🖐 Free

The Grand Theatre at night

Jing'an Si occupies a site used for temples for the last 1,700 years

Nanjing Lu and People's Square

Although competition has arisen, both in Shanghai and in other cities, Nanjing Lu remains China's most famous shopping street.

DISTANCE: 3km (2 miles) **ALLOW:** 1.5 hours (not including stops)

START

PEACE HOTEL
✚ J5 🚇 Nanjing Donglu

END

PEOPLE'S SQUARE
✚ G6 🚇 People's Square

WALK

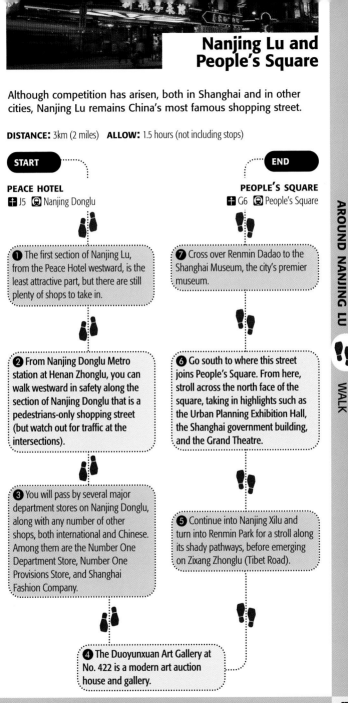

❶ The first section of Nanjing Lu, from the Peace Hotel westward, is the least attractive part, but there are still plenty of shops to take in.

❼ Cross over Renmin Dadao to the Shanghai Museum, the city's premier museum.

❷ From Nanjing Donglu Metro station at Henan Zhonglu, you can walk westward in safety along the section of Nanjing Donglu that is a pedestrians-only shopping street (but watch out for traffic at the intersections).

❻ Go south to where this street joins People's Square. From here, stroll across the north face of the square, taking in highlights such as the Urban Planning Exhibition Hall, the Shanghai government building, and the Grand Theatre.

❸ You will pass by several major department stores on Nanjing Donglu, along with any number of other shops, both international and Chinese. Among them are the Number One Department Store, Number One Provisions Store, and Shanghai Fashion Company.

❺ Continue into Nanjing Xilu and turn into Renmin Park for a stroll along its shady pathways, before emerging on Zixang Zhonglu (Tibet Road).

❹ The Duoyunxuan Art Gallery at No. 422 is a modern art auction house and gallery.

Shopping

CHINA TOURIST SOUVENIR CORPORATION

Huge shop selling handicraft items, imitation antiques and souvenirs from around the country. The advantage here is the large range of merchandise under one roof.

🔲 D6 ✉ Shanghai Exhibition Centre, 1000 Yan'an Zhonglu ☎ 6279 0279 🚇 Jing'an Si 🚌 49, 71

CITY SUPERMARKET

Expats and visitors in town who have perhaps had one Chinese meal too many or are feeling the need for some familiar comfort food flock to the two branches of this sophisticated supermarket for international delicatessen items, familiar brand-name foodstuffs and more.

🔲 E7 ✉ Hong Kong New World Department Store, 939–947 Huaihai Zhonglu ☎ 6474 1260 🚇 Shaanxi Nanlu

CYBERMART

Shanghai celebrates its fascination with things that bleep at this market leader in consumer electronics, which is packed with the latest, the finest and even occasionally the cheapest in everything from USB memory sticks to computers and DVD players.

🔲 G7 ✉ 282 Huaihai Zhonglu ☎ 6390 8008 🕐 Daily 10–8 🚇 Huangpi Nanlu

DONGTAI LU ANTIQUES MARKET

Covering a compact area a few blocks west of the Old Town, the city's most important antiques market has an extensive array of small shops and stalls featuring everything from genuine antiques, through what could best be described as bric-a-brac, to out-and-out junk (even some junk is fake, so let the buyer beware).

🔲 G7 ✉ Dongtai Lu 🕐 Daily 9–5 🚌 13, 42, 63

HUA LIAN

This store was the renowned Wing On Department Store, and in its day, before the war, the latest thing in shopping. It has now been reborn as an international-style shopping center.

🔲 H5 ✉ 635 Nanjing Donglu ☎ 6322 4466 🚇 Nanjing Donglu 🚌 20, 37

ISETAN

Tokyo-based department store selling all the world's latest wares, though concentrating on items from Japan.

🔲 F7 ✉ 527 Huaihai Zhonglu ☎ 5306 1111 🚇 Shaanxi Nanlu 🚌 26, 42, 911

LEI YUNG SHANG

Traditional Chinese medicines may look quaint in the slick setting of Nanjing Lu, but this venerable practitioner has plenty of customers.

🔲 F5 ✉ 719 Nanjing Xilu ☎ 6255 2708 🕐 Daily 8.30am–9pm 🚇 West Nanjing Road

NEW WORLD

From Adidas to Ermenegildo Zegna, by way of Cerruti 1881, Esprit, Lacoste, Swarovski and Versace, to name but a bare-bones few out of hundreds, the New World is nothing if not focused on known international brand names, and fits them all handily into its extensive floor space.

🔲 G5 ✉ 2–68 Nanjing Xilu ☎ 6358 8888 🕐 Daily 10–10 🚇 Renmin Park

PARKSON GROCERY

A Western-style supermarket taking up one floor of the department store of the same name.

🔲 E7 ✉ Basement Level, Parkson Department Store, 918 Huaihai Zhonglu ☎ 6415 6384 🚇 Shaanxi Nanlu 🚌 126, 911, 42

PLAZA 66

Arguably the pick of the malls lining Shanghai's main shopping street, Plaza 66 is the place to

head if money is no object. More than 100 designer brands are represented, from Hermès to Bang & Olufsen.

🅵 E5 ✉ 1266 Nanjing Xilu
☎ 6279 0910 🚇 West Nanjing Road

RAFFLES CITY

This Singaporean-owned mall has won plaudits for being a well-designed and comfortable place to shop. It's especially good for casual clothes, with a good spread of popular chains. There's also a cinema and spa.

🅵 G6 ✉ Xizang Zhonglu
☎ 6340 3600 🚇 Renmin Square

SHANGHAI ARTS & CRAFTS SERVICE CENTER

Jadeware, embroideries, ivory carving, leather goods, carpets, gold and silver in an accessible location adjacent to the Park Hotel and opposite the old racecourse.

🅵 G5 ✉ 190 Nanjing Xilu
☎ 6327 6530 🚌 20, 37

SHANGHAI FASHION COMPANY

Despite the name, this shop, which occupies part of a venerable building that once housed one of Shanghai's original department stores, can't really compete in the fashion stakes with the newest shops retailing chic international styles, but it does have an extensive range of clothes

at moderate prices.

🅵 H45 ✉ 660–690 Nanjing Donglu ☎ 6352 5445
🕐 Daily 9.30am–10pm
🚇 Nanjing Donglu

SHANGHAI FIRST PROVISIONS COMPANY

This large supermarket stocks mainly Chinese products but has a growing range of international brands. It is a good resource for putting together a picnic or for stocking up for days when you don't want to eat out at a restaurant.

🅵 H5 ✉ 720 Nanjing Donglu ☎ 6322 2777
🕐 Daily 9.30am–10pm
🚇 Nanjing Donglu
🚌 20, 37

SHANGHAI FOREIGN LANGUAGE BOOKSTORE

This place has a decent selection of fiction and nonfiction books in English and other languages, and books covering China, its culture and language. The shop also sells CDs and stationery.

CLOTHES

Probably the best place for clothes shopping is the Huaihai Road, the main road of the former French Concession, where several shops specialize in designer clothes imported from Hong Kong, and other designer shops have appeared in the last few years.

🅵 H6 ✉ 390 Fuzhou Lu
☎ 6322 3200 🕐 Daily 9–7
🚇 Nanjing Donglu 🚌 17, 49

SHANGHAI JINGDEZHEN PORCELAIN ARTWARE STORE

Porcelain and handicrafts, many of them from the kilns at Jingdezhen in Jiangxi province.

🅵 F6 ✉ 1175 Nanjing Xilu
☎ 6253 0885 🚇 Jing'an Si
🚌 20, 37

SHANGHAI MUSEUM SHOP

In fact, there are three shops on the southern side of the museum that specialize in books, antiques and antique reproductions.

🅵 G6 ✉ 201 Renmin Dadao
☎ 6372 3500 🕐 Daily 9–5
🚇 Renmin Square 🚌 23

WELLCOME SUPERMARKET

This is an expensive Hong Kong supermarket selling Western and Japanese produce.

🅵 D5 ✉ 1376 Nanjing Xilu
☎ 6279 8018 🚇 Jing'an Si
🚌 37

WESTGATE MALL

Another of the shopping malls that have sprouted along Nanjing Lu. Its stores feature haute couture, street-cred fashion boutiques and other requisites of an upwardly aspiring lifestyle.

🅵 E5 ✉ 1038 Nanjing Xilu
☎ 6218 7878 🕐 Daily 10–10
🚇 West Nanjing Road

Entertainment and Nightlife

CHINA THEATRE

A refurbished venue that puts on performances of opera, dance, theater acrobatics, and more.
➕ H5 ✉ 704 Niuzhuang Lu ☎ 6351 7389 🚇 Renmin Square 🚌 25

D D'S

Spacious place where you can take part in the karaoke and then dance to the latest sounds.
➕ C6 ✉ 322 Huashan Lu ☎ 6248 2251 🕐 6pm–3am 🚇 Jing'an Si 🚌 48

GRAND CINEMA

One of the city's main cinemas, showing Hollywood and Chinese films.
➕ J6 ✉ 216 Nanjing Xilu ☎ 6327 4260 🚌 20, 27

JING'AN HOTEL

Offering quite a step up from the usual piano player or small music combo in the lobby, the Jing'an Hotel lobby is the venue for weekly chamber music concerts by musicians from the highly regarded Shanghai Symphony Orchestra.
➕ C6 ✉ 370 Huashan Road ☎ 6248 1888 ext. 617 🚇 Jing'an Si

KOWLOON CLUB'S LONGBAR DISCO

A joint venture taking up a lot of space in one of the buildings of the old Shanghai Exhibition Centre.
➕ G6 ✉ 1333 Nanjing Xilu ☎ 6279 0279 Ext 7110 🚌 37

MAJESTIC THEATRE

Traditional Chinese opera, music and dance are performed at one of the city's finest old theaters.
➕ E5 ✉ 66 Jiangning Lu ☎ 6217 4409 🚇 West Nanjing Road

MALONE'S BAR

An American-style bar that has been through a few style changes over the years. Weekly film shows (American and European) take place, usually on a Wednesday.
➕ D5 ✉ 257 Tongren Lu ☎ 6247 2400 🚇 Jing'an Si

SHANGHAI CENTRE THEATRE

One of the highlights of the multiuse Shanghai Centre (▷ 46), the theater puts on a varied agenda of Chinese and international music, opera, theater and dance, along with performances by the stellar Shanghai Acrobatic Theatre.

(▷ 46)

CHINESE OPERA

Chinese opera is completely unlike Western opera. Foreigners find it difficult to appreciate at first but it is worth trying at least once. The singing style is falsetto and the action heavily stylized, but overall it is very colorful and can be highly dramatic, especially if battles are staged using acrobatic techniques. Check the local press for performances.

➕ D5 ✉ Shanghai Centre, 1376 Nanjing Xilu ☎ 6279 8614 🚇 Jing'an Si 🚌 20, 27

SHANGHAI CONCERT HALL

This handsome building was built as the Nanking Theatre in 1930. It was moved, brick by brick, 216ft (66m) to its present site in 2004. The 1,200-seat concert hall hosts the Shanghai Symphony Orchestra and visiting artists.
➕ D6 ✉ 523 Yan'an Donglu ☎ 5386 6666 🚇 Renmin Square 🚌 46, 71, 123, 574

SHANGHAI SALLY'S

English-style pub offering pub food, a good range of drinks and games.
➕ E7 ✉ 4 Xiangshan Lu ☎ 6327 1859 🚇 Huangpi Nanlu 🚌 24

STUDIO CITY

A six-screen multiplex at the top of a modern shopping mall. The films are Chinese and international, with some shown in their original English.
➕ E5 ✉ 10th Floor, Westgate Mall, 1038 Nanjing Xilu ☎ 6218 2173 🚇 West Nanjing Road

TIANCHAN YIFU THEATRE

Head to this theater, which was renovated in 2004, for Chinese opera.
➕ G–H6 ✉ 701 Fuzhou Lu ☎ 6351 4668; reservations 6217 2426 🚇 People's Square 🚌 46, 71, 123, 574

Restaurants

PRICES

Prices are approximate, based on a 3-course meal for one person.
$$$ more than 250RMB
$$ 100–250RMB
$ under 100RMB

THE ATRIUM CAFÉ ($$–$$$)
A high-ceilinged, modern restaurant serving a range of foods from different cuisines, from Chinese through to continental European and Middle Eastern. Excellent breakfast buffets, Sunday brunch and Viennese pastries.
➕ C6 ✉ Hilton Hotel, 250 Huashan Lu ☎ 6248 0000 ext.86 ⏰ Breakfast, lunch, dinner 🚇 Jing'an Si 🚌 45

THE CAFÉ ($$)
A spacious, rustic-style hotel café, which is open 24 hours. There is a buffet of European dishes each day, a patisserie and made-to-order omelets, pasta and burgers.
➕ F6 ✉ Equatorial Hotel, 65 Yan'an Xilu ☎ 6248 1688 ⏰ Breakfast, lunch, dinner 🚇 Jing'an Si 🚌 71

E-CAFÉ ($$)
Within the Equatorial Hotel, this café is devoted mainly to pasta dishes and pizzas as well as sublime tiramisu.
➕ C6 ✉ 65 Yan'an Xilu ☎ 6248 1688 ext. 2384 ⏰ Lunch, dinner 🚇 Jing'an Si 🚌 48, 71

FU LIN XUAN ($$–$$$)
The glass-and-wood decor is stylish and the Cantonese seafood is pretty good, though service is variable.
➕ E7 ✉ 37 Sinan Lu ☎ 6372 1777 ⏰ Lunch, dinner 🚇 Huangpi Nanlu 🚌 24

GONGDELIN ($–$$)
A famous vegetarian restaurant. The dishes are imitations of meat (using tofu).
➕ F6 ✉ 445 Nanjing Xilu ☎ 6327 0218 ⏰ Lunch, dinner 🚇 People's Square 🚌 20, 27

JADE BUDDHA TEMPLE ($)
Restaurant serving regional vegetarian dishes in the famous temple.
➕ D3 ✉ 170 Anyuan Lu ☎ 6266 3668 ⏰ Lunch 🚌 24, 105, 106, 112

KATHLEEN'S 5 ($$–$$$)
Set on the fifth floor of the Shanghai Art Museum

SOUP

In the West it is customary to have soup as a starter or appetizer but in China soup is generally served toward the end of the meal as a sort of "digestif," and on informal occasions is also a way of helping to finish remains in the rice bowl. At formal functions such as banquets, soup is served in a separate bowl.

(and with a glassed-in rooftop terrace), this smart restaurant serves American-based cuisine that roams the world for elements to mix and match, with local influences. Brunch is served from 11am on weekends.
➕ G6 ✉ 325 Nanjing Xilu ☎ 6327 2221 ⏰ Mon–Thu 11.30am–midnight, Fri 11.30am–1am, Sat–Sun 11am–1am 🚇 Renmin Park 🚌 46, 71, 123, 574

LONG BAR ($$)
Decorated to give a taste of prewar Shanghai, this is essentially a bar (with juke box), which serves substantial Western and Chinese snacks.
➕ G6 ✉ Shanghai Centre, 1376 Nanjing Xilu ☎ 6279 8268 ⏰ Lunch, dinner 🚌 20, 37

MEI LONG ZHEN ($$)
This is in the former Communist Party headquarters serving food in Huaiyang, Sichuan and Shanghainese styles Deep-fried *gui* (fish), tofu dishes and cold shredded jellyfish are on the menu.
➕ G6 ✉ 1081 Nanjing Xilu ☎ 6253 5353 ⏰ Lunch, dinner 🚌 37

PUCCI ($)
Good fresh pastries, doughnuts, biscuits and dairy products.
➕ F7 ✉ 1st Floor, Isetan, 527 Huaihai Zhonglu ☎ 5306 1111 ⏰ Shopping hours 🚇 Shaanxi Nanlu 🚌 26, 42, 911

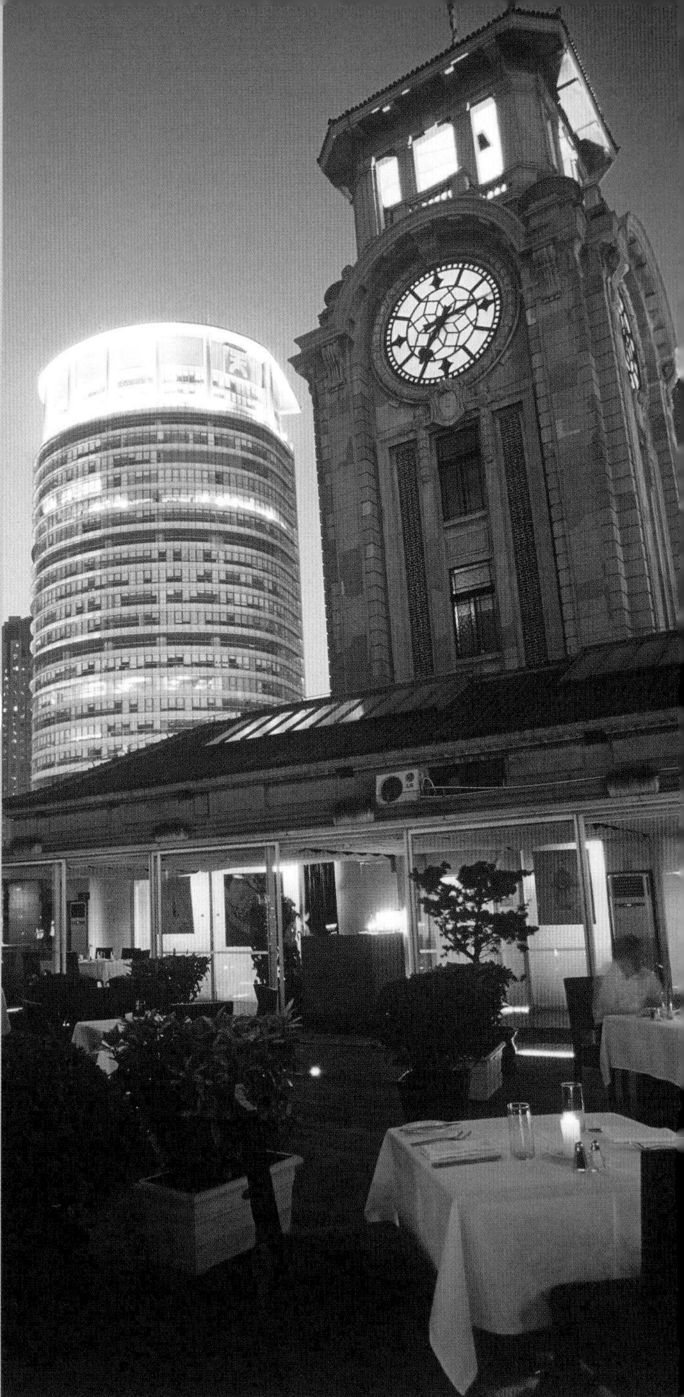

Stretching north from Renmin Lu on the edge of the Old City to Suzhou Creek, the Bund is Shanghai's premier promenade. From here you have a stunning view across the water to Pudong's glittering towers.

WUSONG LU

Hanyang Lu
Yangqu Lu
Minhang Lu
Hongkou Lu
Liyang Lu
Nanxun Lu
Xi'an Lu
Dongchangzhi Lu
Lu
Shangiu Lu
Yongding Lu
Lushun Lu
Liling Lu
Machang Lu
Branch
Tangqu Lu
Changzhi Lu

DAMING LU
DONGDAMING   **LU**

Astor
House
Hotel
Huangpu   Minhang Lu   Nanxun

International
Passenger
Terminal

H u a n g p u

K   L

The Bund/Waitan

HIGHLIGHTS

- Garden Bridge
- Former British Consulate
- Russian Consulate
- Astor House Hotel
- Broadway (Shanghai) Mansions

Suzhou Creek has long been a feature of the Shanghai landscape. It came to represent much that was unattractive in the city's rush to develop but now it is a sign of how the city is cleaning up its act.

TIP

- It is more pleasant these days to stroll the riverside paths along either bank. The occasional sorry-looking green scraps of yore have been joined by riverside parks, gardens and pedestrian walkways, with more to follow in the years to come.

The colonial period Suzhou Creek separated the British and American Concession, and the creek banks close to the Huangpu River have some architectural survivors from this time. The Broadway Mansions Hotel at 20 Suzhou Beilu is housed in an art deco masterpiece that was the Shanghai Mansions (1934). Also on the north bank, the Astor House Hotel (▷ 63), at 15 Huangpu Lu, dates from 1846. The twin-span steel Waibaidu (Garden) Bridge, which crosses over the creek alongside Huangpu Park (▷ 63) dates from 1907 and replaced wooden bridges on

Clockwise from left: Vessels line the sides of the creek and traffic passes along the middle; selling bicycle registrations near Suzhou Bridge; Zhongshan Donglu; a new apartment block on the creekside; Suzhou Creek artists' quarter

the same site. After serving as a seamen's hostel, the old Russian Consulate building at 20 Huangpu Lu again houses the Russian Consulate.

Troubled waters From its source in Tai Hu (Lake Tai) close to Suzhou, the creek flows east through some of China's most polluted territory before debouching into the Huangpu River at the north end of the Bund. By 1998, when the first clean-up measures were introduced, Suzhou Creek's once crystal-clear water had become a black open sewer. Those who lived beside the creek—a fate reserved for the poor—could not open their windows in summer so bad was the smell. The Suzhou Creek Rehabilitation Project has changed things for the better. More needs to be done, but fish are returning and the expectation is that by 2010 they should feel at home in the water.

THE BASICS

✚ West and north from K5
✉ Suzhou Nanlu and Suzhou Beilu
🚇 Nanjing Donglu, Xinja Lu
🚌 20, 42, 55, 65

The Bund

陈 毅
1901–1972

HIGHLIGHTS

● Panoramic views
● Waterfront European-style buildings
● Boat trips on the Huangpu River (▷ 60)

TIP

● The Bund shows different faces of itself during the day: Early morning tai chi practitioners give way to rush-hour crowds, then a period of calm before the lunchtime and afternoon strollers emerge. Evening, the time for leisure crowds, is followed by those out to view the lights.

Traveling by ship from Europe or America in the 1930s, the expatriate's first view of Shanghai would have been the waterfront street known as the Bund, a grand slice of the colonial world that is still impressive today.

Waitan The Bund (a word of Anglo-Indian origin, meaning "waterfront" or "embankment") is now known as Waitan or Zhongshan Donglu and runs along the Huangpu River from Suzhou Creek in the north to Yan'an Lu in the south. The buildings that line it date from the early 20th century and are entirely Western in style. The Bund is where modern Shanghai began and it remains the hub of the city. A "must do" activity is to stroll the Bund after dark when the illuminated waterfront and the view to Pudong create a memorable view.

Clockwise from left: Flag flying atop the Customs Houses clock tower; statue of Chen Yi, the first mayor of Shanghai; the Bund viewed from the Riverside Promenade; tai chi exercises; a bronze lion outside the Hong Kong and Shanghai Bank

The buildings Although changes have been made—the trams have gone, as have the old "go-downs," or warehouses, and statues of foreigners—the Bund would be instantly recognizable to a 1930s resident. A walk from south to north would begin with the Shanghai Club at No. 3 (and later the Dong Faeng Hotel), which claimed to have the longest bar in the world. The domed building at No. 12 was the Hong Kong and Shanghai Bank, built in 1921. Next door, surmounted by a clock once known as Big Ching, is the Customs House of 1927 with beautiful ceiling mosaics inside. Next to the main building of the Peace Hotel (▷ 62) on the corner of Nanjing Lu (Nanking Road) is the Bank of China (1937). No. 27 was the head-quarters of Jardine Matheson, one of the early companies to prosper from the opium trade, and No. 32 was the old British Consulate.

THE BASICS

✚ J6–K5

✉ Zhongshan Donglu

🍴 Various restaurants and cafés

🚌 20, 42, 55, 65

♿ None

♿ Various

Huangpu Riverboat Tour

TOP 25

- The busy port
- Confluence with the mighty Yangtze
- Great views of the Pudong commercial district and the new developments on Fuxing Island

- Should a cruise on the Huangpu take up more time or money than you can afford, try instead the cross-river ferries, which you can think of as affording a cheap microcruise on the river.

The Huangpu and Yangtze rivers are the original reasons for Shanghai's prosperity. A river cruise along the Huangpu will show aspects of this huge city you might not otherwise see.

Two rivers The Yangtze is the longest river in China. Rising in the Tibetan Plateau, it meanders right across the country, passing through several provinces, and most famously, the Three Gorges. The Huangpu, only 68 miles (110km) in length, runs from Lake Tai and empties into the Yangtze River some 17 miles (28km) downstream. Its average width through the city is 1,300ft (400m) and its average depth 26ft (8m). Large ships were able to enter the wide mouth of the Yangtze, make the short journey up the Huangpu and unload their cargoes at the wharves along the

Clockwise from left: A plaque showing the level of the Huangpu flood in 1997; looking across the river from the Bund to Pudong; a nighttime view across to Pudong with the Oriental Pearl TV Tower prominent to the left of center

Bund. The goods were transported by barges along Suzhou Creek and then along the network of canals for distribution throughout China.

Touring the Huangpu Boat tours leave from the Bund, a little way north of the Peace Hotel (▷ 62). If you travel first class, the journey, which lasts about three and a half hours, is very comfortable. Refreshments are provided and, during the return journey, there is often a performance of some kind, usually magic or acrobatics. You first pass Suzhou Creek on the left, overlooked by Shanghai Mansions, and then the International Passenger Terminal, while to your right is Pudong. Then comes the Yangshupu Power Plant and Fuxing Island, where Chiang Kai Shek made his last stand before fleeing to Taiwan. Finally you meet the Yangtze, before returning to the city.

THE BASICS

www.shpjyl.com
🚇 L5
✉ Boat leaves from Bund pier, close to Huangpu Park
☎ 6374 4461
🕐 Cruises depart daily every 2 hours or so 9am–10pm
🍴 Bar on board ship
🚌 20, 42, 55, 65
♿ None
💷 Moderate—tickets through CITS or from a kiosk close to the pier
❓ Performances often given on river cruise

Peace Hotel

The Peace Hotel alongside the Bank of China (left); the hotel's Old Jazz Band (right)

Even if you don't stay at the Peace Hotel, you should drop in one evening to have a drink and to hear its famous jazz band. This relic from Shanghai's extravagant past is one of the city's symbols.

The Sassoons Of the many families of Sephardic Jews that flourished in prewar Shanghai, the best known is the Sassoon family. They fled an intolerant Baghdad in the 18th century to make a fortune in Bombay and then proceeded to buy warehouses in Shanghai. Successive generations invested in the port, but it was Victor Sassoon who built the well-known landmark on the Bund now known as the Peace Hotel. Though it represents the hated era of foreign domination, many new skyscrapers ape its distinctive pyramidical roof design.

The Cathay There had been a Sassoon House on the Bund for some time, but Victor Sassoon had visions of a skyscraper as a modern business headquarters and wanted to include a fabulous hotel into the bargain. Today's Peace Hotel, originally the Cathay, dates from 1930, with art deco ironwork and high ceilings inside and looking somewhat like a smaller Empire State Building outside. The lowest four floors were reserved for offices; the remainder were given over to what Victor hoped would be the finest hotel in the East. It had the best technology and service that the period could offer, while the Horse & Hounds Bar became the most fashionable rendezvous in the city. Today the Peace Hotel incorporates the old Palace Hotel from across Nanjing Lu.

THE BASICS

www.shanghaipeacehotel.com

➕ J5

✉ 20 Nanjing Donglu

☎ 6321 6888

🕐 Daily

🍴 Café, bar and restaurant on premises

🚇 Nanjing Donglu

🚌 37, 42, 55, 65

♿ None

💰 Free but expensive to stay there

❓ Jazz band performs in the evening

HIGHLIGHTS

● Classic art deco architecture

● Jazz in the evening

More to See

ASTOR HOUSE HOTEL

Now restored as a fancy hotel (▷ 110), this building just across the bridge at the northern end of the Bund, opposite the Russian Consulate, was once one of the city's finest hotels.

🚹 K5 ✉ 15 Huangpu Lu ☎ 6324 6388 🕙 Daily 🚌 28 🐾 None 🖐 Free

BUND SIGHTSEEING TUNNEL

This psychedelically lit tunnel runs under the water from the Bund, opposite Nanjing Donglu, to the Pudong shore. You board an unmanned miniature train car for the four-minute ride, during which a sound-and-light show unfolds, with images projected on the walls of the tunnel.

🚹 J6–K6 ✉ Zhongshan Dongyilu 🕙 Mon–Thu 8am–10.30pm, Fri–Sun 8am–11pm (to 10pm daily Nov–Mar) 🚇 Nanjing Donglu 🚌 65 🖐 Moderate

HUANGPU PARK

At the northern end of the Bund near the bridge, this is the infamous park where a notice was said to forbid entry to "Dogs and Chinese" (the wording was not exactly like that in fact). It is a pleasant park overlooking the river, with an ugly monument, beneath which a small museum with exhibits about old Shanghai.

🚹 K5 ✉ The Bund 🕙 Summer daily 6am–10pm; winter 6–6 🚌 65 🐾 None 🖐 Free

METROPOLE HOTEL

This small skyscraper hotel was known for its restaurants before 1945. Soong Qing-Ling and Chiang Kai Shek had their wedding banquet here.

🚹 J6 ✉ 180 Jiangxi Zhonglu ☎ 6321 3030 🕙 Daily 🚇 Nanjing Donglu 🚌 37, 42, 55, 65 🐾 None 🖐 Free

SHANGHAI MUSEUM OF NATURAL HISTORY

This central museum has an interesting collection of items relating to Chinese flora and fauna. There are stuffed animals, photographs and dinosaur bones.

🚹 J6 ✉ 260 Yan'an Donglu ☎ 6321 3548 🕙 Daily 9–5 🚇 Nanjing Donglu 🚌 71 🐾 Few 🖐 Inexpensive

Early morning exercises in Huangpu Park

A street artist in Huangpu Park

The Bund

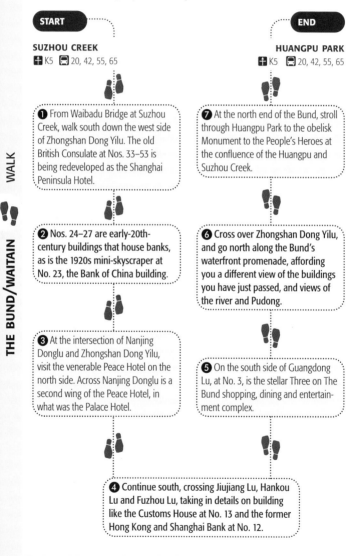

The Bund was where the story of modern Shanghai began, and its colonial-era buildings are still an attraction.

DISTANCE: 0.5 miles (1km) **ALLOW:** Up to 1 hour

START

SUZHOU CREEK
🚇 K5 🚌 20, 42, 55, 65

END

HUANGPU PARK
🚇 K5 🚌 20, 42, 55, 65

① From Waibadu Bridge at Suzhou Creek, walk south down the west side of Zhongshan Dong Yilu. The old British Consulate at Nos. 33–53 is being redeveloped as the Shanghai Peninsula Hotel.

⑦ At the north end of the Bund, stroll through Huangpu Park to the obelisk Monument to the People's Heroes at the confluence of the Huangpu and Suzhou Creek.

② Nos. 24–27 are early-20th-century buildings that house banks, as is the 1920s mini-skyscraper at No. 23, the Bank of China building.

⑥ Cross over Zhongshan Dong Yilu, and go north along the Bund's waterfront promenade, affording you a different view of the buildings you have just passed, and views of the river and Pudong.

③ At the intersection of Nanjing Donglu and Zhongshan Dong Yilu, visit the venerable Peace Hotel on the north side. Across Nanjing Donglu is a second wing of the Peace Hotel, in what was the Palace Hotel.

⑤ On the south side of Guangdong Lu, at No. 3, is the stellar Three on The Bund shopping, dining and entertainment complex.

④ Continue south, crossing Jiujiang Lu, Hankou Lu and Fuzhou Lu, taking in details on building like the Customs House at No. 13 and the former Hong Kong and Shanghai Bank at No. 12.

CAITONGDE DRUGSTORE

Specializes in traditional Chinese herbs and cures.
🔲 J5 ✉ 320 Nanjing Donglu ☎ 6350 4740 🚇 Nanjing Donglu 🚌 37, 42, 55, 65

CHINESE ANCIENT BOOKSTORE

Antiquarian books, paintings, stationery and items required for calligraphy.
🔲 J6 ✉ 424 Fuzhou Lu ☎ 6322 3453 🚇 Nanjing Donglu 🚌 17, 49

DUO YUN XUAN ART STUDIO

Calligraphy, paintings, stationery, rubbings of ancient carvings and seals.
🔲 K6 ✉ 422 Nanjing Donglu ☎ 6466 2806 🚌 37

LAO ZHOU HU CHENG CHINESE WRITING BRUSH AND INKSTICK STORE

This shop supplies the items needed for traditional Chinese painting and calligraphy—brushes, inkstones and ink slabs, for example.
🔲 J5 ✉ 90 Henan Zhonglu ☎ 6323 0924 🚇 Nanjing Donglu 🚌 66

SHANGHAI ANTIQUE & CURIO STORE

Established shop selling porcelain, jewelry, silk embroidery, paintings and other antique items.
🔲 J6 ✉ 192–240 Guangdong Lu ☎ 6321 4697 ⏰ Daily 9–5 🚇 Nanjing Donglu 🚌 66

BAR 505

Re-created German Bräuhaus—brick-and-stone interior and copper vats—serving good beer and snacks from a good location in a hotel on the east Nanjing Lu.
🔲 K6 ✉ Hotel Sofitel Hyland, 505 Nanjing Donglu ☎ 6351 5888 ⏰ 7am–1am 🚇 Nanjing Donglu 🚌 37

BAR ROUGE

High up amid the setting of Bund 18 is the setting for the coolest cocktail bar in town, its atmosphere ramped up by name DJs after midnight and its nighttime outlook a big draw by itself.
🔲 J6 ✉ 18 Zhongshan Dong Yilu ☎ 6339 1199 ⏰ Mon–Thu 3pm–2am, Fri–Sat 3pm–4am; special brunch Sat–Sun noon–4pm 🚇 Nanjing Donglu 🚌 37, 42, 55, 65

GLAMOUR BAR

This place lives up to its aspirations and reputation. A Chinese take on thickly encrusted art deco, it does creative cocktails and vibrant views of the Bund. Sister establishment M on the Bund next door is every bit as glamorous.
🔲 J6 ✉ 7th Floor, 20 Guangdong Lu ☎ 6350 9988 ⏰ Daily 5pm–2 or 3am 🚇 Nanjing Donglu 🚌 37, 42, 55, 65

NEW YORK NEW YORK

One of the most popular discos in town.
🔲 K5 ✉ 146 Huqiu Lu ☎ 6321 6097 ⏰ 8pm–5am 🚌 21

SHANGHAI NIGHT BAR

The glassed-in setting of the Peace Hotel's (▷ 62) leafy but chic rooftop bar affords a fine view of the ebb and flow of life on the Bund.
🔲 J5 ✉ Peace Hotel, 20 Zhongshan Dong Yilu ☎ 6321 6888 ⏰ Daily 10am–11pm 🚇 Nanjing Donglu

Restauts

PRICES

Prices are approximate, based on a 3-course meal for one person.
$$$ more than 250RMB
$$ 100–250RMB
$ under 100RMB

BUND 12 ($–$$)

A great opportunity to look inside of one of the Bund's venerable landmark buildings. The café, on the second floor, is a miniature masterpiece of period refurbishment, with original marble fireplace and art deco light fittings. A balcony with terrace tables overlooks the courtyard. The menu includes sandwiches, salads, pasta, pizzas, cakes and fresh fruit juices.
✚ J6 ✉ Room 226, 12 Zhongshan Donglu (Bund) ☎ 6329 5896 ⏰ Lunch, dinner ⏏ Nanjing Donglu 🚍 37, 42, 55, 65

CAFÉ DE LA SEINE ($–$$)

Essentially a bar, but one that serves snacks such as filled baguettes, cakes, croissants and a few other French-influenced dishes. Excellent location by the Huangpu River.
✚ K6 ✉ 236 Zhongshan Dong 1-Lu (Bund) ☎ 6323 9379 ⏰ Lunch, dinner 🚍 22, 126, 42, 55

FEST BREW HOUSE ($–$$)

A beerhall that sells the only home-brewed beer in Shanghai, as well as serving the dishes to go with it—baked fish, oxtail soup, or pork Lyonnaise.
✚ J6 ✉ 11 Hankou Lu ☎ 6321 8447 ⏰ Daily 11–11 ⏏ Nanjing Donglu 🚍 49

FIFTY HANKOU LU ($$)

In a spacious prewar building, which used to be a bank, that's now decorated in Indonesian style, and well-placed near the Bund, this restaurant serves in an eclectic mix of European and Asian dishes as well as afternoon tea. The laksa lemak, lamb korma and Makhani chicken are the specialties here.
✚ J6 ✉ 50 Hankou Lu ☎ 6323 8383 ⏰ Lunch, dinner ⏏ Nanjing Donglu 🚍 49

MAO RESTAURANT ($$–$$$)

Good local cooking in the Sofitel Hyland Hotel, just 15 minutes' walk from the Bund.

DESSERT

For most Westerners, even those who adore Chinese food, the one thing missing from a meal is something truly sweet at the end. Desserts are not a big feature of Chinese meals but banana cooked in a toffee sauce, and Eight Treasure Rice—a delicious, if slightly heavy concoction of rice, honey and fruit—are especially good.

✚ J5 ✉ 505 Nanjing Donglu ☎ 6351 5888 ⏰ Lunch, dinner ⏏ Nanjing Donglu 🚍 37, 42, 55, 65

MOSIAC ($–$$)

This attractive deli, on the second floor of the Sofitel Hyland Hotel, sells cakes, biscuits and pastries. It's about a 15-minute walk from the Bund.
✚ J5 ✉ Sofitel Hyland Hotel, 505 Nanjing Donglu ⏰ All day ⏏ Nanjing Donglu 🚍 37, 42, 55, 65

SHANGHAI GARDEN ($$–$$$)

In the old Metropole Hotel, this restaurant serves Cantonese as well as Shanghainese food. In its day the Metropole was said to serve the best food in town and it is still excellent.
✚ J6 ✉ 180 Jiangxi Zhonglu ☎ 6321 3030 ⏰ Lunch, dinner ⏏ Nanjing Donglu 🚍 37, 42, 55, 65

WHAMPOA CLUB ($$$)

Run by one of Shanghai's celebrity chefs, Jereme Leung, this ineffably smart restaurant on the fifth floor of the glitzy Three on the Bund center, offers a contemporary, fusion take on Shanghai cuisine to tasteful effect.
✚ J6 ✉ Three on the Bund, 3 Zhongshan Yilu (entrance at 17 Guangdong Lu) ☎ 6321 3737 ⏰ Daily 11.30–2.30, 5.30–11 ⏏ Nanjing Donglu 🚍 37, 42, 55, 65

Old Shanghai contains the fragrant Yu Garden, the idiosyncratic Huxingting Tea House and several venerable temples, while the Nanshi district affords a sense of escape into a less frantic way of life.

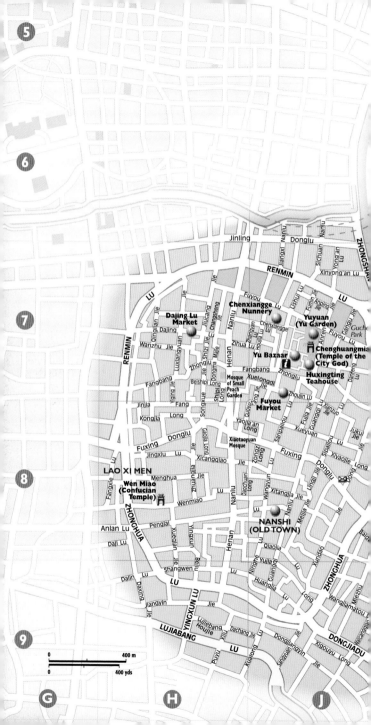

Huxingting Tea House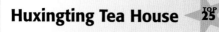

HIGHLIGHTS

● Charming building in entertaining location
● Cooling on hot days

TIP

● When the waiter or waitress refills your tea cup, tapping the index and second fingers of your right hand is a traditional way to indicate "thank you" for being served tea–the gesture represents the kowtow that everyone had to do in the presence of the emperor.

The delightful old teahouse, in its watery setting in the middle of a lake, is the focal point of the Old Town. It fits in with the China of popular imagination, a China that has all but disappeared.

Tea drinking Tea is widely produced throughout central and southern China and is also widely consumed in everyday life–taxi drivers often keep a jar with them, half filled with leaves to which boiling water is added throughout the day; there will probably be tea in your hotel room; and when people meet, or at an official function, tea will certainly be served at some point. In the past, however, every town had several teahouses, where conversation was an adjunct to an appreciation of good teas. However, an appreciation of fine teas and the art of tea drinking in its ceremonial form,

Clockwise from top left: A suited waiter in the teahouse; people negotiating the Nine Zig-Zag Bridge to the teahouse; visitors to Shanghai enjoying tea; the teahouse illuminated at night; relaxing with tea and snacks

where such matters as the quality of the water used are much considered, has largely vanished.

Huxingting The Huxingting Tea House, surrounded by a small lake, is truly the hub of the Old Town. Its precise origins are not entirely clear, but it dates from some time during the Ming dynasty, was renovated as a brokerage house in 1784, and became a teahouse in 1856. It was originally part of both the Temple of the City God (▷ 75) and Yuyuan (▷ 74). As Shanghai prospered, parts of the garden, including the teahouse, were purchased by local merchants who used it as a meeting place for conducting business. A building of great charm, it is approached via the Nine Zig-Zag Bridge, over waters glittering with goldfish. Inside you may drink good-quality tea from traditional teapots—refreshing on hot summer days.

THE BASICS

➕ J7
✉ 257 Yuyuan Lu
☎ 6373 6950
🕐 Daily upstairs 8.30am–10pm and downstairs 5.30–10
🍴 Plenty of restaurants nearby, in the Old Town
🚌 11, 14, 26
♿ None
💲 Moderate
❓ Tea ceremony performed in the evening

Old Town

HIGHLIGHTS

● A hint of the atmosphere of old China
● Excellent snack food and shops

TIP

● Most visitors to the Old Town focus on its northern section, around Yuyuan and the Huxingting Tea House. But there's much more to the district than this, and if anything the other parts are more authentic.

One of the unexpected pleasures of Shanghai is to discover, amid the high-rise modernity, an old Chinese town—the original Shanghai. In its narrow streets you can absorb something of the atmosphere and bustle of traditional China.

History Until the Treaty of Nanking in 1842, Shanghai was a moderately important walled town concentrated in the area now called Nanshi. The walls were pulled down in 1911 to provide better access for shops and traders, but even now the area is self-contained and the route of the old walls can be traced along Renmin Lu and Zhonghua Lu. You can still find a single wide street with narrow alleys branching from it. The middle of the town was dominated then, as it is today, by the Huxingting Tea House (▷ 70), the

Clockwise from top left: Collectibles at Dongtai Lu antiques market; traditional clothes in Dongjiadu Fabric Market; renovated stores; the Bird and Flower Market; a small tailoring shop; steamed dumplings ready for sale; an old city building

Yuyuan (▷ 74) and the Chenghuang Miao, or Temple of the City God (▷ 75).

Today Although there have been many changes, with the addition of new shops designed in the traditional Chinese style, the old Chinese town retains its prewar atmosphere. There are many small shops that specialize in items such as tea, walking sticks and even wigs. The newer shops sell jewelry and antiques. Perhaps the most enjoyable pastime is to snack on delicious freshly made dumplings at one of the restaurants. The two principal entrances to the town are from Fuyou Lu, beside the Lao Fandian restaurant (▷ 79), and through the arch of the Temple of the City God, off Fangbang Zhonglu. Once you are inside, any lane will eventually bring you to the central area and the Huxingting Tea House.

THE BASICS

➕ H7–J9
🍴 Plenty of restaurants in the area
🚌 11, 14, 26
♿ None
🎟 Free

Yuyuan

TOP 25

A willow overhangs a pond in the garden; detail of a building

Shanghai does have its surprises. Hidden from casual observation in the heart of the Old Town is one of the finest classical gardens remaining in China.

The Pan family The Yuyuan, or Yu Garden, has a very long history. In its current incarnation it was created in the mid-16th century by a certain Pan Yunduan as an act of filial affection for his father. Pan, a native of Shanghai who had been in public service in Sichuan Province, must have been a wealthy and influential figure in the city, for the garden takes up almost 5ha (12 acres), a large chunk of the Old Town. By the time it was completed in 1577, however, Pan's father had died, and although additions were made to the garden from time to time, it suffered from neglect. Twice in the 19th century it was used as headquarters—in 1842 by the British Land Force and in the 1850s by the Small Swords Society, dedicated to the restoration of the Ming dynasty.

Today's garden The Yu Garden exemplifies the classic Ming garden, where rock gardens, bridges and ponds surround pavilions and corridors to create an illusion of a natural landscape. In reality, although the materials used are the work of nature, the design is very obviously the work of man. But what is important in this garden is the "harmony of scale" its beauty lying in the intricate design, which in the past would have permitted tranquil contemplation in a comparatively small area. An unusual feature is the sculpted dragon that curls around the top of the garden wall.

More to See

BAI YUN SI

The Taoist White Cloud Temple, built in 1883, lies outside the west gate in the Old Town on Fangxie Lu. It is the birthplace of the Quanzhen Sect of Taoism. Inside, a statue of the Jade Emperor is the object of worshippers' veneration. Regular ceremonies are accompanied by traditional Tao music using gongs and flutes.

➕ G8 ✉ No. 8, Lane 100, Xilin Houlu
🕐 Daily 8–5 🚌 11, 18, 23, 24 ♿ None
✋ Inexpensive

CHENGHUANG MIAO (TEMPLE OF THE CITY GOD)

The temple has been reconstructed more than 20 times since it was founded in 1403, but its popularity with devotees, especially those praying for wealth and prosperity, remains undiminished. The hall of the City God is to the rear of the building, beyond the inner courtyard, where you may see red-robed trainee monks, a reminder that this is a working temple.

➕ J7 ✉ 24a Fangbang Zhonglu (at Yu Garden) 🕐 Daily 8.30–4.30 🚌 11, 14, 26 ♿ None ✋ Inexpensive

CHENXIANGGE NUNNERY

This is the largest Buddhist temple in China. It originally belonged to the Pan family, who built Yuyuan, and takes its name from an eaglewood statue of the Buddha, which gives off a resinous scent in damp weather.

➕ J7 ✉ 2a Chenxiangge Lu 🕐 Daily 7–4
🚌 11, 24, 26 ♿ None ✋ Inexpensive

DAJING LU MARKET

Dajing Lu is a teeming market street where you can still see a communal way of life that is fast disappearing in other parts of the city. The area's lanes and alleyways are lined with terraces of Shikumen courtyard houses, dating from the early 20th century.

➕ H7 ✉ 150–160 Dajing Lu 🕐 Daily 8–8
🚌 11, 14, 26 ♿ None ✋ Free

DONJIADU CATHEDRAL

Built by Spanish Jesuits in 1853 as the Saint Xavier cathedral, in a style reminiscent of Iberian colonial

Statue of Confucius at Wen Miao Temple (▷ 76)

Worshippers at Chenxiangge Nunnery

baroque, which makes it worthwhile to see even if the interior is closed, Dongjiadu is the oldest Catholic church in Shanghai and stands outside the southeastern edge of the Old Town, a few blocks from the Huangpu River. It is a working church, with Mass in Chinese said daily.

✚ K9 ✉ 175 Dongjiadu Road 🚇 Nanpu Daqiao 👪 Free

FUYOU MARKET

The most famous market for antiques in Shanghai takes place on a Sunday just outside the Old Town. Until 1998, several dozen mobile stalls lined Fuyou Lu to provide the largest antiques market in the city—many of the stallholders would arrive before dawn to ensure a good position along the road. Now the market has a permanent home here on Fangbang Zhonglu, close to Henan Nanlu. Prices can be quite high here, so haggling is a must.

✚ J7 ✉ 457 Fangbang Zhonglu 🕐 Daily 9–5 🍴 Restaurants 🚌 11, 14, 26 🚫 None 👪 Free

WEN MIAO

This Confucian Temple is to be found to the south of the Temple of the City God and close to the site of the old West Gate. As well as the temple dedicated to Confucius, there is a small market and swings for children.

✚ H8 ✉ 215 Wenmiao Lu 🕐 Daily 8.30–4.30 🚌 11, 14, 26 🚫 None 👪 Inexpensive

YU BAZAAR

Despite appearances—ceremonial gateways, rosewood lanterns, traditional pagodas with sloping eaves— the Yu Bazaar was constructed in the 1990s. This is one of the best places in Shanghai to shop for gifts and souvenirs, though not for genuine antiques. (Haggling is expected, but you may be able to negotiate a better price in the smaller shops on Fangbang Zhonglu, once you have an idea of the going rate.) Stilt walkers, acrobats and street artists entertain the crowds on summer weekends.

✚ J7 ✉ Streets around Yuyuan 🕐 Daily 7–4 🚌 11, 14, 26 🚫 None 👪 Free

Chops for sale at the Yu Bazaar

The entrance to Yu Bazaar

Old Town

Many old buildings remain in the Nanshi district, Shanghai's formerly walled old town, and you will see some of them on this walk.

DISTANCE: 2.2 miles (1.5km)   **ALLOW:** 1 hour (not including stops)

START

DONGMEN LU
J8 20, 42, 55, 65

END

HENAN LU
H7 11, 14, 26

❶ From Dongmen Lu, the site of the old east gate to the Chinese town, close to the Huangpu River. Walk westward and pass Waixangua Jie (Salty Melon Street), with its local street market.

❷ Continue to Zhonghua Lu and cross the street to enter Fangbang Zhonglu.

❸ Continue past a variety of shops until an old Chinese arch appears to the right. This is the entrance to the Temple of the City God.

❹ Go through the arch and make your way among the shops and restaurants until you come to the lake and the Huxingting Tea House, or Mid-Lake Pavilion, near the entrance to the Yuyan (Yu Garden).

❼ Return to Jiujiaochang Lu and continue past stands and shops to Fangbang Zhonglu. Turn right until you reach the permanent antiques market on the right, at the corner of Henan Lu.

❻ Turn left here and left again into Jiujiaochang Lu. A street on the right (Chenxiangge Lu) takes you to a small neighborhood temple, the Chenxiangge Nunnery.

❺ Bear right around the lake and then turn left to wander among the narrow streets before bearing right to leave this area and emerge into Fuyou Lu.

WALK

Shopping

SHOPPING

OLD TOWN/NANSHI

FRIENDSHIP STORE

While adjusting to competition from nearby department stores, this large branch of the Friendship Store chain continues to retail interesting antiques, including quality porcelain and cloisonné, along with handmade fabrics and other craft items. Prices are generally on the expensive side and you can't bargain them down, but many visitors looking for a decent souvenir prefer this approach to the lottery of a street market.

➕ J6 ✉ 68 Jinling Donglu ☎ 6337 3555 🕐 Daily 9.30–9.30 🚇 Nanjing Donglu 🚌 71

FUMIN SMALL COMMODITIES MARKET

Just outside the Yu Garden, this building houses small shops that sell a wide variety of Chinese products.

➕ J7 ✉ 223–225 Fuyou Lu 🕐 Daily 9am–10pm 🚇 Nanjing Donglu 🚌 11, 14, 26

HUABAO BUILDING ANTIQUES MARKET

Housed in the basement of a building close to the Yu garden, this is one of the city's best sources of antiques.

➕ J7 ✉ 265 Fangbang Zhonglu 🕐 Daily 9am–10pm 🚇 Nanjing Donglu 🚌 42, 64, 86

OLD SHANGHAI TEAHOUSE

Not only can you drink Chinese teas here and peruse antique teapots and tea services, you can also buy many different brands of tea, including the famous Dragon Well tea from Hangzhou, along with teapots, cups, saucers and more at the shop on the ground floor.

➕ J7 ✉ 385 Fangbang Zhonglu ☎ 5382 1202 🕐 Daily 8.30am–11pm 🚇 Nanjing Donglu 🚌 42, 64, 86

BUYING ANTIQUES

It is illegal to export anything older than 150 years. A red seal on an antique will tell you that it is genuine and exportable. There are so many shops and market stands selling antiques that the seal of approval may be absent, and if it is, there's no sure-fire method of knowing what you are buying other than to really inspect the object in question. Some imitations are of a very high standard but are often marked on the bottom as being authentic reproductions. This is information the salesperson is unlikely to volunteer, but if you like the item it will still be cheaper than the real thing!

SHANGHAI OLD STREET

Not nearly as old as its given name implies, having been redeveloped as recently as 1999, the eastern segment of Fangbang Zhonglu at least creates a convincing illusion of being old, thanks to its small shops selling antiques, crafts, bric-a-brac and tea.

➕ J7 ✉ Fangbang Zhonglu 🚇 Nanjing Donglu

SHANGHAI SOUTH BUND FABRIC MARKET

The former Dongjiadu Market moved to these new indoor premises in 2006. There is a huge selection of raw textiles to choose from (wool, silk, linen, cotton and so on)—expect to pay in the region of 20–30RMB per metre. You can also have clothes made to measure here, although very little English is spoken.

➕ J9 ✉ 399 Lujiabang Lu ☎ 6377 5858 🕐 Daily 8–6 🚇 Nanpu Daqiao 🚌 4

SILK MUSEUM

This emporium on the edge of the Yu Bazaar sells all manner of silk products, from shirts and jackets to quilts and embroidered pyjamas.

➕ J9 ✉ 125 Jiujiaochang Lu ☎ 6355 0312 🕐 Daily 9–8 🚇 Nanjing Lu 🚌 11, 14, 26

Restaurants

PRICES

Prices are approximate, based on a 3-course meal for one person.
$$$ more than 250RMB
$$ 100–250RMB
$ under 100RMB

Yuyuan lake. Celebrity status has made the food a little touristy and the bills higher, but the overall experience is worthwhile.
🔢 J7 ✉ 115 Yuyuan Lu ☎ 6328 0602 🕐 Daily 7am–1am 🚇 Nanjing Zhonglu

HUXINGTING TEA HOUSE ($)

There's nowhere in Shanghai quite like this venerable teahouse (▷ 70) for experiencing a taste of Old China, even if great popularity has brought the crowds.
🔢 J7 ✉ 257 Yuyuan Lu ☎ 6373 6950 🕐 Daily 8.30am–10pm 🚇 Nanjing Donglu 🚌 11, 14, 26

LAO FANDIAN (SHANGHAI OLD RESTAURANT; $$–$$$)

Something of an institution, this modernized version of an old restaurant (the name means old restaurant) serves Shanghai dishes (including noodles, and seafood according to the season) and is conveniently situated in the Old Town.
🔢 J7 ✉ 242 Fuyou Lu, Old Town ☎ 6328 2782 🕐 Lunch, dinner 🚇 Nanjing Donglu 🚌 11

LU BO LANG ($$)

International movers and shakers, celebrities and ordinary folks alike pile into this signature Old Town traditional eatery on the edge of the

MAGNIFICENT RESTAURANT ($$)

For anyone who wants to experience the street animation of the Old Town yet prefers to escape from its noise and bustle during mealtimes, this air-conditioned hotel restaurant, which serves Shanghainese cuisine, is a good choice.
🔢 H8 ✉ Magnificent International Hotel (2nd Floor), 381 Xizang Nanlu ☎ 5383 8588 🕐 Daily 7am–9pm 🚌 17, 18, 23

LOCAL SNACKS

One of the specialties of the region is Ningbo or "pigeon egg" dumplings, little balls of sticky rice enclosing a delicious sweet *osmanthus* paste. Another snack is *zhong zhi*, sticky rice with meat wrapped in a lotus leaf. To find these and other delicious snacks, stop in the Old Town—both in the area of the Huxingting Tea House and on the streets around it where there are a large number of small restaurants ($) and stalls. 🔢 H6 🚌 26

NAN XIANG ($–$$)

The best place in the city to try *xiaolongbao* (Shanghai-style steam dumplings). These are stuffed with various fillings: vegetables, crab, pork. All three floors here are usually busy, so be ready to wait for a table.
🔢 K7 ✉ 85 Yuyuan Lu ☎ 6355 4206 🕐 Lunch, dinner 🚌 11, 14, 26

OLD SHANGHAI TEA HOUSE ($)

Escape the hustle and bustle of the Yu Bazaar to this small island of peace and sanity. The teahouse is awash with 1920s memorabilia, with everything from biscuit tins to old telephones. The staff wear long Mandarin gowns or silk *qipaos* and serve the teas on lacquered trays. Snacks of sour plums, muskmelon seeds and quail eggs come with the tea.
🔢 K7 ✉ 385 Fangbang Zhonglu ☎ 5382 1202 🕐 Daily 8.30–11 🚌 42, 64, 86

XIAO SHAOXING ($$)

There's a relaxed atmosphere here, with modern furnishings and gentle live music in the evenings. The menu offers reasonably priced dishes from all over China. Sample the crab and noodles claypot and *yangcen* (fried rice).
🔢 K7 ✉ 96 Sichuan Nanlu ☎ 6328 3992 🕐 Lunch, dinner 🚌 126

OLD TOWN/NANSHI   RESTAURANTS

A rambling district north of Suzhou Creek, Hongkou incorporates the International Concession. It later became a haunt of liberal and revolutionary writers, artists and intellectuals.

Duolun Lu
Cultural Street

HIGHLIGHTS

● Shikumen houses
● Shops selling antiques, art and period bric-a-brac
● Bustling modern Chinese character and colonial-period mansions
● Atmospheric cafés

TIP

● The proximity of Duolun Lu and Lu Xun Park to each other and their complementary character should add up to a decent day out in old Hongkou.

This sensitively restored pedestrian street of Shikumen houses and pebble-dash villas, once the haunt of China's radical writers, is lined with art galleries, curio shops, teahouses and terrace cafés.

Shops If you take Metro line 3 to Dong Baoxing Lu, turn right out of the station then left onto Sichuan Beilu, you will come to Duolun Lu after about 5 minutes' walk. The street was actually created as an "instant attraction" in the late 1990s, but that fact doesn't detract much from its character today. The formerly artificial district has taken on a genuine life of its own. Many of the shops here specialize in collectables: Mao badges at No. 183, chopsticks at No. 191, porcelain at No. 185, while "1933" is a trove of antique clocks and far more along the zigzag street.

From left to right: Hongde Church; a statue of Charlie Chaplin at the Old Film Café; people strolling along Doulun Lu Cultural Street

Culture You can photograph the old brick doorways, the clock tower and the former Great Virtue Church (No. 59) with its curious mixture of Chinese and Western styles. The church now houses small craft shops, or you can check out the exhibitions in the Shanghai Duolun Museum of Modern Art.

Literary connections Bronze statues dotted along the street commemorate the coterie of radical liberal and Communist writers who met here in the 1930s, and who, between them, created a new Chinese literature, far removed in spirit from the fossilized tropes of the past. The most famous of them, Lu Xun, had a profound influence on Chinese literature and is still revered today. You can find out more about him by visiting the museum in Lu Xun Park.

THE BASICS

✚ K2
✉ Outside the main gate of Lu Xun Park at the corner of Jiangwan Lu and Tain'ai Lu
🚇 Dong Baoxing Lu
🚌 4, 9, 18, 21
🍴 Cafés and teahouses

Shanghai Duolun Museum of Modern Art
www.duolunart.com
✉ 27 Duolun Lu
☎ 6587 6902
🕐 Tue–Sun 10–6
♿ Inexpensive

Lu Xun Park

The boating lake (left); locals playing Chinese chess (right)

HIGHLIGHTS

● Lu Xun's mausoleum and Memorial Hall
● Boating lake

TIP

● Hongkou Stadium adjoins Lu Xun Park on the north side, making it possible to combine a soccer match with a visit to the park.

If you want a window on Shanghai life away from the city center, then try to get to Lu Xun Park, where local people come to find refuge and meet friends away from their crowded housing conditions.

Hongkou Hongkou is the area north of Suzhou Creek (the Wusong River), a large part of which was the former American Concession before it merged with the British Concession in 1863. The accepted date of its foundation is 1848, when a church mission was established here. After the Americans, Hongkou became home to many Japanese, earning the soubriquet of Little Tokyo. Here also was the Mixed Court (administered by a Chinese magistrate and a foreign assessor), the Russian post office and various risqué cabarets.

Lu Xun Lu Xun Park, originally laid out in 1905, has a large lake with rowing boats for hire in the summer. Shrubs and flowers attract butterflies, while the open-air setting draws amateur painters and opera singers. Every autumn there are chrysanthemum shows. Above all, the park is known for its associations with the eminent writer Lu Xun, who lived in Hongkou from 1927 until his death in 1936, and is best known for *The True Story of Ah Q*, whch lampoons the Chinese character. His house, at 9 Dalu Xinchun, Sanyin Lu, on a street just outside the park, is open to the public and illustrates what housing was like in the Japanese part of Shanghai. In the park there is a museum dedicated to his life, as well as his mausoleum and his likeness cast in bronze.

Shopping

CARREFOUR
Good French-based hypermarket selling Western groceries and household items at reasonable prices.

🔲 M2 ✉ Zhongshan Park Shopping Center, 1018 Chang Ning Lu ☎ 6555 8078
🚇 Zhongshan Gongyuan

EUTORIA
Not many shoppers can afford genuine Ming Dynasty porcelain, but a reproduction might be possible. You'll find these, along with fine modern Jingdezhen vases and other pieces here.

🔲 K2 ✉ Unit 702, 1915 Sichuan Beilu ☎ 5696 7878
🚇 Dongbaoxing Lu 🚌 13, 17, 18, 19, 21, 70

GUO CHUN XIANG CURIOSITY SHOP
Some of the objects on sale in this cluttered little shop are antiques, but "collector's items" might be a better way to describe the curios, minor pieces, pop culture items, Mao badges, toys and Chinese bric-a-brac from as recently as the 1960s.

🔲 K2 ✉ 179–181 Duolun Lu ☎ 5696 3948
🚇 Dongbaoxing Lu 🚌 13, 17, 18, 19, 21, 70

SHANGHAI SPRING DEPARTMENT STORE
A modern six-floor area store, at the corner of Wuchang Lu, where prices are significantly less than those in the flagship department stores on Nanjing Lu and Huaihai Lu. It retails food, clothing, consumer electronics, jewelry, and more.

🔲 J4 ✉ 521 Sichuan Beilu ☎ 6357 0090 🚌 17, 19, 21, 65, 66

Restaurants

PRICES
Prices are approximate, based on a 3-course meal for one person.
$$$ more than 250RMB
$$ 100–250RMB
$ under 100RMB

HONG DONG KOREAN RESTAURANT ($$)
This restaurant has a clean-lined, almost Scandinavian look, although diners sit on comfy wicker chairs while enjoying spicy dishes from the peninsula.

🔲 K2 ✉ 239 Duolun Lu ☎ 6540 3636 🕙 Daily 10–10 🚇 Dongbaoxing Lu 🚌 13, 17, 18, 19, 21, 70

KAM BOAT RESTAURANT ($$)
Located in the towering Best Western New Century Hotel Shanghai this stately Cantonese restaurant is a somewhat staid yet reliable performer. The seafood dishes are fine.

🔲 K2 ✉ 1111 Liyang Lu ☎ 3608 4999 🕙 Daily 6.30–10pm 🚇 Dongbaoxing Lu 🚌 13, 17, 18, 19, 21, 70

TAN HOTPOT ($–$$)
Squeamish folks who become faint at the very thought of tucking into a complete fish head needn't apply for a table in a restaurant where this is the chef's specialty (though it's far from being the only dish). The fish in question is silver carp. Appropriately for a Sichuanese restaurant, it stands on Sichuan Road.

🔲 J3 ✉ 2222 Sichuan Beilu ☎ 5696-2476 🕙 Daily 10am–midnight
🚇 Dongbaoxing Lu

There's nowhere else in China quite like Pudong district. It's really a city with 1.5 million inhabitants which sprang up from farmland in less than 20 years. Its towers are a grand sight from the Bund.

Sights	**92–96**	Top 25	**TOP 25**
Shopping	**97**	Oriental Pearl Tower ▷ **92**
Restaurants	**97–98**	Pudong Skyscrapers ▷ **94**

上海八音盒珍品陈列馆
The Shanghai Gallery of Antique Music Box and Mechanical Work

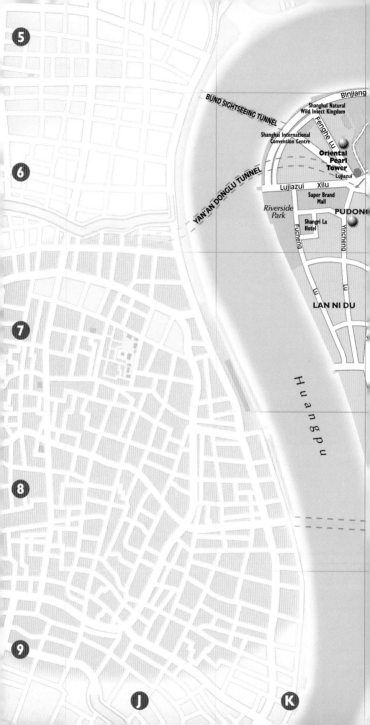

5

6

7

8

9

BINJIANG

BUND SIGHTSEEING TUNNEL

Shanghai Natural
Wild Insect Kingdom

Shanghai International
Convention Centre

**Oriental
Pearl
Tower**

Lujiazui

YAN'AN DONGLU TUNNEL

Lujiazui   Xilu

Super Brand
Mall

Riverside
Park

PUDONG

Shangri La
Hotel

Fucheng

Yincheng

LAN NI DU

H u a n g p u

J

K

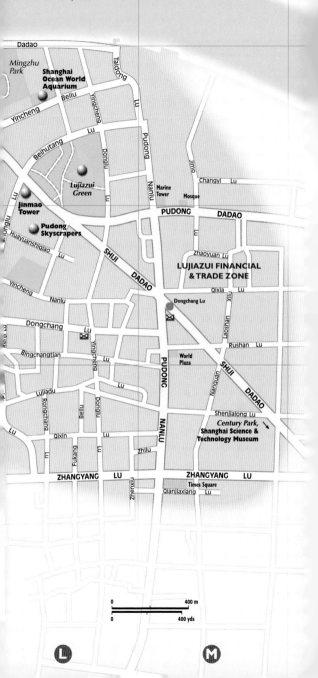

Oriental Pearl Tower

HIGHLIGHTS

● Wonderful views across the city
● A glimpse into the future of Shanghai

TIP

● If you are in Shanghai for a short time you should take in the view from the tower whatever the atmospheric conditions are. Should you be in town on a haze-free day, make it a priority to get up there and enjoy the view.

Not too many years ago the tallest building in China was still the Park Hotel on Nanjing Lu. Now it has been dwarfed by many others, above all by this communications tower with an extra-ordinary view across the city.

Pudong New Area Pudong, across the river from the Bund, is the fastest growing urban area in the world, already as large as Shanghai itself. Until the early 1990s it was full of rundown factories and offices and farmland, accessible only by ferry. The only reason to go there would have been for the view across the river to the Bund.

Oriental Pearl Tower Pudong now has plenty to offer, as it exemplifies a China that is changing before your eyes. Still hard to beat, however, are

Views of the Oriental Pearl Tower, the tallest building in Asia; the expanding city as seen from the tower (below left)

the views back across the river to the Bund and the giant Oriental Pearl Tower, currently the tallest building in Asia and the third in the world, its top truly disappearing into the clouds. Though not a building of great beauty, the panorama over Shanghai and beyond, from a viewing area half-way up, is splendid. The tower is 1,535ft (468m) high and in 1995 began broadcasting shows through nine television channels and 10 FM channels. To the Chinese it is known as "two dragons playing with a pearl" reflecting the Chinese way of describing things in fanciful ways. The tower houses the intriguing Shanghai Municipal History Museum. The city's history is short by Chinese standards, and the main focus of the museum is the colonial period that gave Shanghai, among other things, the buildings on the Bund on the other side of the river.

THE BASICS

✚ K6
✉ 2 Lujiazui Lu
☎ 5879 1888
🕐 8am–9.30pm
🚇 Lujiazui
🛥 Ferry from opposite Yan'an Donglu
♿ Moderate
🖐 Moderate
❓ Jazz band in café

Shanghai Municipal History Museum

☎ 5879 3003
🕐 Daily 9–9
🖐 Inexpensive

HIGHLIGHTS

● Views from the Jinmao Tower's 88th floor observation deck
● Jinmao Tower's Cloud 9 bar
● Grand Hyatt Hotel's restaurants

TIP

● Pudong's large-scale development is due to be complete by 2010 (and then further development is likely). So for some time there will be the opportunity to view the final pieces in the master-plan's jigsaw.

Pudong New Area is larger than Shanghai itself, and its financial district is the fastest-growing in Asia. There are more than 6,000 skyscrapers here, most less than a decade old, the headquarters of international banks and Fortune 500 companies.

Jinmao Tower A Chinese pagoda inspired the design of this soaring structure, built by the same firm of architects as the Sears Tower in Chicago, and completed in 1999. It is now the second tallest in China and the fourth tallest in the world at 1,380ft (420m), and on a clear day there are spectacular views of the metropolis from the observation deck on the 88th floor. To get there, enter from the podium building next door—the elevator will whisk you to the top at a stomach-

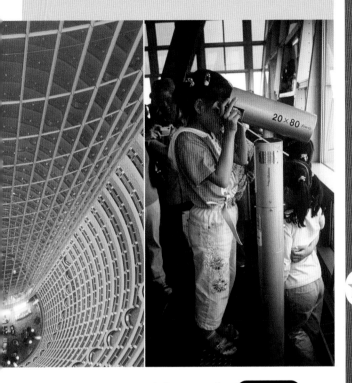

churning 9ft (2.75m) per second. There are retail outlets selling souvenirs, and you can send a postcard direct from the post office. Return after dark when the city is illuminated to enjoy more views and the gourmet restaurants of the Grand Hyatt hotel (▷ 112), which occupies floors 53 through 87. Cloud 9 on the top floor claims to be the world's highest bar.

Shanghai World Financial Center With a shape reminiscent of a giant bottle opener, this unfinished building next to the Jinmao is due to outdo it—with 95 floors and a height of 1,614ft (492m). Construction hit the doldrums in the 1990s, but work was resumed in 2003 and the estimated completion date is 2008. As well as offices, it too will house a hotel, along with shops and an observatory.

THE BASICS

Jinmao Tower
www.jinmao88.com
✚ L6
✉ 2 Shiji Dadao
☎ 5047 6688
🍴 Restaurants and cafés
🚇 Lujiazui
🚌 81, 82, 85, 583, 621, 623, 776, 778, 797, 870, 872, 983
🎟 Free

Shanghai World Financial Center
www.shanghaihills.com
✚ L5

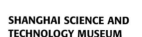

More to See

CENTURY PARK

In heavily urbanized, high-tech Pudong, a park that covers 346 acres (140ha) is a resource worth being grateful for. It's large enough to accommodate a central lake where visitors can rent small boats, ornamental gardens, pavilions, children's play areas, and more. And a river, the Zhangjiabang, runs through it.

🔁 Off map, east of M8 ✉ Huamu Lu and Jinxiu Lu ☎ 3876 0588 🕐 Daily 7–6 (to 5 mid-Nov to mid-Mar) 🚇 Shiji Gongyuan 🚻 Good 💷 Inexpensive

LUJIAZUI GREEN

In the shadow of the Jinmao Tower (▷ 94) and the Oriental Pearl Tower (▷ 92), this large, tree-fringed garden with a lake at its heart is popular with the workers of Pudong's many offices. It is the most convenient venue for all the things the Shanghainese like to do in their parks, everything from merely strolling to practicing tai chi and enjoying kite-flying.

🔁 L6 ✉ Lujiazui Lu ☎ 24 hours 🚇 Lujiazui 🚻 Good 💷 Free

SHANGHAI SCIENCE AND TECHNOLOGY MUSEUM

www.sstm.org.cn

This state-of-the-art museum, the largest of its kind in Asia, opened to popular acclaim in 2001. The scope of the exhibition extends from biodiversity and space exploration to design innovation and digital technology.

🔁 Off map at M8 ✉ 2000 Shiji Dadao ☎ 6862 2000 🕐 Tue–Sun 9–5.15 🚇 Science and Technology Museum 🚻 Few 💷 Moderate

SHANGHAI OCEAN WORLD AQUARIUM

www.aquarium.sh.cn

There are 13,000 creatures. Predictably, it's the sharks, penguins and spider crabs that draw the crowds, but this is a rare opportunity to see endangered Chinese species. You can walk along the longest glass tunnel in the world (509ft/155m).

🔁 L6 ✉ 158 Yincheng Beilu ☎ 5877 9988 🕐 Daily 9–6 (to 9 Jul and Aug); animal feeding times around 10.30 and 3 🚇 Lujiazui 🚻 Few 💷 Expensive

The beautiful flower beds at Century Park

Shopping

CHIA TAI DEPARTMENT STORE

This formerly exclusive branch of the Thai department store chain on four floors of the Super Brand Mall had a shaky start as shoppers were slow to take to Pudong, but that has changed now that it stocks a broader range of goods and as the parent mall has reached a wider target audience.

🔽 K6 ✉ 168 Lujiazui Lu ☎ 6887 7888 🕐 Daily 10–10 🚇 Lujiazui

WAL-MART SUPERCENTER

The US chain store's third branch in Shanghai is at the south end of the

Pudong's main development zone, close to the approach road to and from the Nanpu Bridge.

SLOW START

Pudong has been slow to take off as a shopping district. This is because shoppers have been slow to change their habits. Now, as more people settle in Pudong, and as the effects of the generally high level of disposable income of people living and working in Pudong have kicked in, the picture is changing. Retailers, large and small, cheap and expensive, are moving in.

🔽 Off map at L9 ✉ 252–262 Linyi Beilu ☎ 5094 5881 🕐 Daily 9am–10pm 🚇 Lujiazui

YATAI SHENGHUI SHOPPING CENTRE

In addition to its wide range of modestly priced goods, from clothing to jewelry, the shopping mall below the metro station at the Shanghai Science and Technology Museum (▷ 96) has developed a reputation as the place to go to buy imitation branded goods.

🔽 Off map at M9 ✉ 2002 Shiji Dado (Century Boulevard) ☎ 5094 5881 🕐 Daily 10–10 🚇 Science & Technology Museum

Restaurants

PRICES

Prices are approximate, based on a 3-course meal for one person.
$$$ more than 250RMB
$$ 100–250RMB
$ under 100RMB

DANIELI'S ($$–$$$)

Ultra-urbane Italian cuisine is served in a dark, cherrywood ambience near the top of the St Regis Hotel. Look for innovative dishes made with homemade pastas, truffles, porcini mush-

rooms and more on the plate, and superb views.

🔽 Off map at M9 ✉ St Regis Hotel, 889 Dongfang Lu ☎ 5050 4567 🕐 Lunch, dinner 🚇 Dongfang Lu

JADE ON 36 ($$$)

This exceptional restaurant on the 36th floor of the Grand Tower is a gem of intercontinental, multicultural fusion. The setting is a modernist take on Chinese themes.

🔽 K6 ✉ Pudong Shangri-La Hotel, 33 Fucheng Lu ☎ 6882 3636 🕐 Daily 6–10.30pm 🚇 Lujiazui

RED CHOPSTICKS ($$–$$$)

This breezy place serves the kind of noodle dishes hurried diners around China wolf down—with a bit more expense but at a bit more class but the principle remains.

🔽 M8 ✉ InterContinental Pudong Shanghai Hotel, 777 Zhangyang Lu ☎ 5835 6666 🕐 Lunch, dinner 🚇 Dongchang Lu

Some of Shanghai's attractions, though far from the center, are still well within the city limits. Such places of interest are liable to be swamped with city-dwellers on weekends but are well worth visiting on weekdays.

HIGHLIGHTS

● Active temple
● Beautiful jade carvings

TIP

● Photographing either of the Jade Buddha statues in the temple is not permitted. Don't try to sneak a picture. Aside from the lack of respect this shows, it might easily generate a "vexed" reaction from the monks—Buddhist monks aren't supposed to get angry, but being vexed seems to be acceptable.

The busiest and most famous of Shanghai's temples stands among high-rise buildings and small factories. The reason for, and highlight of, a visit is the jewel-covered Buddha in the library, one of two jade Buddhas within the temple.

The temple The Jade Buddha Temple—or Yu Fo Si—was established in 1882 by a monk from the holy mountain of Putuoshan, in southern China, to house the jade Buddha figures. The temple was abandoned after the fall of the Qing dynasty in 1911, then restored between 1918 and 1928. Closed again in 1949, it was saved from destruction during the Cultural Revolution only through the intervention of Prime Minister Zhou En Lai. Although the temple is not of great architectural merit, it is an impressive example of the South

Clockwise from top left: Lighting candles from an open flame; a young woman raises a lighted candle; three Buddhas in the temple complex; worshippers at prayer in the temple; dragon detail on the facade; a huge incense burner in the countyard

Chinese style, especially the roof of the main hall with its steeply raised eaves and decorative figurines. The temple is particularly worth visiting on the first and fifth days of each lunar month, holy days that attract many worshippers.

The Jade Buddhas After visiting the main prayer halls with their array of gaudy Heavenly Kings and Bodhisattvas, it is time to see the temple's highlights, two jade statues brought from Burma by Abbott Wei Ken. Each is carved from a single piece of creamy white jade. They are housed separately. The first is a 3ft (1m)-long reclining Buddha, the position adopted by Buddha at the moment of death. The more beautiful figure is in the library; almost 6.5ft (2m) high, it weighs around 2,200lb (1,000kg) and is encrusted with semiprecious stones.

THE BASICS

⊞ D3
✉ 170 Anyuan Lu, Putuo
☎ 6266 3668
🕐 Daily 8–5
🍴 Excellent vegetarian restaurant
🚌 24, 105, 106, 112
♿ None
💰 Inexpensive
❓ Regular services

Shanghai Zoo

Birds in the zoo (left
and right); a young
red panda in his
enclosure (opposite)

This is more enlightened than many Chinese zoos and provides an opportunity to see some of China's many rare or unique indigenous species. The zoo is near the airport.

Improving conditions The animals here have more space than is the case in many Chinese zoos, but not all that much more. This combined with the penchant of some visitors to bait the animals may take some of the pleasure out of a visit. Nevertheless, like all zoos it can be both fun and educational for children, and there are play areas scattered around. As the authorities become more aware of the facility's shortcomings and acquire the resources to do something about them they have been making significant improvements, particularly in the area of creating naturalistic habitats. The zoo cooperates with international programs to preserve rare and endangered species.

Panda stars Needless to say, the pandas—both giant and lesser pandas—are the stars of the show, and their compound is the best laid-out of all, covering an area of some 1,435sq ft (1,200sq m). It has an indoor and an outdoor area, with a rockery, a pond and trees. But pandas are far from being the zoo's only species. There are some 620 in total, ranging from butterflies to Asian elephants, and coming from all continents. Among them are Brazilian wolves, African chimpanzees, penguins, peacocks, tigers, koala bears, a polar bear, golden-haired and squirrel monkeys, gorillas, South American buffalo and David's deer.

Excursions

THE BASICS

Distance: 40 miles (64km) southwest of Shanghai

✚ Off map to southwest

✉ 6 miles (10km) west of Qingpu town

🍴 Restaurants and cafés

🚌 4 from outside Shanghai Stadium, Xujiahui (Metro: Shanghai Stadium)

DIANSHAN HU

At Dianshan Hu (Lake) there are all sorts of leisure activities—sailing from the marina, a water-sports park, swimming pools, a golf course—and the Grand View Garden, a re-creation of the garden that features in the classic Chinese novel, _Dream of Red Mansions_.

An excursion to Dianshan might include a visit to Qingpu, the county seat, with the Qushui Garden (Crooked Water Garden). The garden was constructed in 1745 and includes a lake, rockeries, pavilions and covered corridors. Close to Qingpu is the town of Zhujiajiao with its canals and old streets. From here to the lake is only 7.5 miles (12km). Shangta is the center of the Dianshan Lake Scenic Area.

THE BASICS

Distance: 25 miles (40km)

✚ Off map to southwest

✉ 6 miles (10km) north of Songjiang town

☎ 5765 1521

🕐 Daily 9–5

🍴 Restaurants and cafés nearby

♿ Few

🚌 1 from outside Shanghai Stadium, Xujiahui (Metro: Shanghai Stadium)

🎫 Free

SHE SHAN

She Shan is a hill about 64 miles (25km) southwest of Shanghai. At its summit, surprisingly, is an imposing, redbrick Catholic church known as "Our Lady of China," where Mass continues to be celebrated in Latin.

Its origins go back to the mid-19th century when a wave of xenophobia led to the construction of a small chapel on the remote hillside. An acting bishop of Shanghai, later forced to take refuge here, vowed that in return for protection he would build a church (the current one dates from 1925). May is a time for pilgrimages when streams of people climb the hill paths, which represent the Via Dolorosa (the route Jesus took to his crucifixion). Next to the church is an observatory established by Jesuit scientist-priests in 1900 for astronomical and geomagnetic research. A radio telescope on the site is engaged in the international VLBI (Very Large Baseline Interferometry) project.

Shanghai caters to all, but there's far more choice in luxury and mid-range hotels than there is in budget lodgings and in expensive hostels. Even so, if you are looking for a good-quality hotel, it's usually best to book ahead.

Introduction

Shanghai is top-heavy with high-end hotels, which are appearing at the rate of three or four a year. These are primarily geared to business travelers and have a high occupancy rate, so if you want to stay you should reserve ahead. By contrast there is a serious shortage of budget accommodations, especially in downtown areas.

Variety of Accommodations
Prices are fast approaching European levels and are set to increase as the 2010 Shanghai Expo looms into view. What Shanghai is strong on is hotels with character, whether on account of historical associations, like the Peace or Tiayuan Villa, or because of their architectural interest, like the Hengshan Moller Villa. While prices are often quoted in dollars on the internet, it is perfectly acceptable to pay in RMB.

Location
Shanghai is a vast, sprawling city that's far from easy to get around quickly or comfortably. While public transport is cheap by Western standards, the Metro is usually busy and buses can be both crowded and hard to figure out. Taxis, which also are relatively inexpensive, may be the preferred option, but fares can add up if you go everywhere by taxi. So it may turn out to be a false economy, in energy if not in money, to forego a more expensive hotel in an area that's close to where you want to be.

STARS IN THEIR COURSES

The hotel star rating system employed in China can often be a reliable guide to what you can expect from a hotel, but not always, and may even be misleading in some cases. The nationally determined five-star category generally means what it says, though many hotels that are a decade or two old have never seen any modernization or upgrading, or even a lick of paint, since they were built. Four- and three-star hotels might have been "assisted" to their status by a "sympathetic" local official. Two- and one-star hotels can be surprisingly dowdy and may even have safety issues.

Budget Hotels

BROADWAY MANSIONS

This ziggurat-like hotel stands just beyond the northern end of the Bund. It has a number of restaurants, including a Japanese one, a business center, a beauty salon, billiard room and shopping arcade.
🛏 L5 ✉ 20 Bei Suzhou Lu
☎ 6324 6260 🚌 65

DONGHU

www.donghuhotel.com
This reasonably priced hotel in the heart of the old French Concession occupies a prewar building that had links with the gangster Du Yuesheng. It has several restaurants (Sichuan and Cantonese), swimming pool and tennis courts.
🛏 D7 ✉ 70 Donghu Lu
☎ 6415 8158 🚇 Shaanxi Nanlu 🚌 44, 49

EAST ASIA HOTEL

Old-style building in an excellent location, providing inexpensive, simple rooms. A host of restaurants are available–Shanghai, Cantonese and French–plus a business center and shopping mall.
🛏 H5 ✉ 680 Nanjing Donglu ☎ 6322 3223
🚇 Renmin Square 🚌 37

HENGSHAN

www.hotelhengshan.com
Old modernized hotel in the southwest of the city. Several restaurants (including one serving French cuisine, and others offering Sichuan and Shanghai styles), business center, sauna, gym and supermarket.
🛏 D8 ✉ 534 Hengshan Lu
☎ 6437 7050 🚇 Hengshan Lu 🚌 42

JIN JIANG YMCA HOTEL

www.ymcahotel.com
Good central location and reasonably priced rooms. Gym, business area and a couple of restaurants.
🛏 H7 ✉ 123 Xizang Nanlu
☎ 6326 1040 🚇 Nanjing Donglu 🚌 17, 18, 23

METROPOLE

www.metropolehotel-sh.com
Close to the Nanjing Lu and the Bund, this hotel in a prewar building is comfortable and a good value. Beauty salon, business center and gym.
🛏 J6 ✉ 180 Jiangxi Zhonglu
☎ 6321 3030 🚇 Nanjing Donglu 🚌 37, 42, 55, 65

PACIFIC HOTEL

Excellent position on Nanjing Lu, this hotel has a piano bar, two restaurants (Western and Fujian) and a business center.
🛏 J6 ✉ 104 Nanjing Xilu
☎ 6327 6226 🚇 Renmin Park 🚌 20, 27

PARK HOTEL

www.parkhotel.com.cn
Classic old prewar skyscraper, modernized a little garishly. Excellent location and facilities, which include a business area, shopping arcade, beauty salon and several restaurants.
🛏 G5 ✉ 170 Nanjing Xilu
☎ 6327 5225 🚇 Renmin Park/People's Square
🚌 20, 37

SEVENTH HEAVEN

Distinctive prewar building on Nanjing Lu at reasonable prices. Rooms are fairly well equipped while facilities include a business center, clinic, post office and a number of restaurants including Cantonese and Sichuan.
🛏 H5 ✉ Nanjing Donglu
☎ 6322 0777 🚇 People's Square 🚌 27

Mid-Range Hotels

ASTOR HOUSE HOTEL

www.pujianghotel.com
Formerly one of the best options for the budget-conscious traveler, the Astor has been refurbished and gone upscale. It is just beyond the north end of the Bund.

➕ J5 ✉ 15 Huangpu Lu
☎ 6324 6388 🚇 Nanjing Donglu 🚌 28

CITY

www.cityhotelshanghai.com
What this 1980s tower block lacks in character, it more than makes up for in location, near Jing'an Temple and the Shanghai Exhibition Center and within striking distance of the French Concession. Rooms are pleasant and airy, and the staff are courteous.

➕ E6 ✉ 5–7 Shaanxi Nanlu
☎ 6255 1133 🚇 Shaanxi Nanlu

CROWNE PLAZA

www.shanghai.crowneplaza.com
Reasonably good location in the western part of the city and with all the good-value facilities associated with this chain. Several restaurants, a well-regarded pub, Charlie's (▷ 31), a delicatessen, indoor swimming pool, sauna and tennis club.

➕ A7 ✉ 400 Panyu Lu
☎ 6280 8888 🚇 Hongqiao Lu 🚌 76

CYPRESS

www.jinjianghotels.com
About 1 mile (2km) from Hongqiao Airport and connected by a free shuttle bus, this modern hotel stands in extensive gardens that give a sense of being in the country—even to the extent of being able to fish in a small lake. The rooms are functional but attractive.

➕ Off map ✉ 2419 Hongqiao Lu ☎ 6268 8868
🚌 4, 57, 48, 91

EQUATORIAL HOTEL

www.equatorial.com
High-rise hotel, not far from the western part of Nanjing Lu, with a steak house, Italian, Japanese and Cantonese restaurants, and a 24-hour café (▷ 51). Also a gym, pool, sauna, and tennis and squash courts.

➕ C6 ✉ 65 Yan'an Xilu
☎ 6248 1688 🚇 Jing'an Si 🚌 71

JING AN HOTEL

Good location close to where the western portion of Nanjing Lu meets the Yan'an Road. The modernized former "Haig Apartments" has restaurants specializing in seafood and Shanghai cooking, a health facility, post office, beauty salon and business center.

➕ C6 ✉ 370 Huashan Lu
☎ 6248 1888 🚇 Jing'an Si 🚌 45, 48

JIN JIANG

Historic prewar hotel in the old style in the former French Concession, close to Huaihai Lu. All twin bedrooms. Several restaurants, a 24-hour coffee shop and a number of good shops.

➕ E7 ✉ 59 Maoming Nanlu
☎ 6258 2582 🚇 Shaanxi Nanlu 🚌 26

JINRONG HOTEL

www.jinronghotel.com
Plush hotel with 245 rooms which is located close to the railway station. Facilities include a business center, clinic, beauty salon, ticket reservation service and Chinese restaurants.

➕ G2 ✉ Gonghexin Lu
☎ 5115 5000 🚇 Shaanxi Huochezan 🚌 46, 95, 108, 114

MARRIOTT HONGQIAO

www.marriott.com/shaqi
This family-friendly hotel in a pleasant residential area of west Shanghai offers excellent facilities at

reasonable prices. Handy for Hongqiao Airport, it is also close to the Yan'an Expressway with fast transit to the center. Rooms are spacious and tastefully furnished, and there's a gym and sauna.
➕ Off map ✉ 2270 Hongqiao Lu ☎ 6237 6000
🚌 911, 925, 936

NOVOTEL ATLANTIS
www.novotel.com
For all that it mimics the typical model of a large, business-oriented tower hotel, its ownership by a French chain affords the Atlantis some refreshing design and service touches. It's a bit isolated, but four restaurants, three bars, a pool and other amenities, including kids' activities, compensate.
➕ Off map ✉ 728 Pudong Dadao ☎ 5036 6666
🚇 Dongchang Lu

OCEAN HOTEL
Good location overlooking the Huangpu River, not too far from the Bund. A revolving restaurant at the top serves Sichuan cooking; disco, shopping arcade and recreation center.
➕ M5 ✉ 1171 Dongdaming Lu ☎ 6545 8888 🚌 28

OLD HOUSE INN
www.oldhouse.com
Be transported back to the Shanghai of the 1930s: Stay in this quaint, beautifully renovated lane house in the former French Concession. All 12

rooms are furnished in Ming dynasty style with canopy beds, carved wooden cabinets and fine silk drapes. The restaurant serves typical Shanghainese cuisine.
➕ C6 ✉ 16, Lane 351, Huashan Lu ☎ 6248 6118
🚇 Jing'an Si

PEACE HOTEL
www.shanghaipeacehotel.com
The classic Shanghai hotel on the Bund. Modernization has not been completely sympathetic but the hotel's position and historical associations are hard to beat. Business center, gym, sauna, billiards, restaurants and the famous jazz bar.
➕ J5 ✉ 20 Nanjing Donglu ☎ 6321 6888 🚇 Nanjing Donglu 🚌 27

LODGING IN PUDONG
The Pudong New Area on the east bank of the Huangpu River, which is in effect a new city, has a virtually complete absence of anything that remotely resembles traditional Chinese style. Twenty-first century Chinese style is something else. The fact that everything is shiny, international and new, and works, makes Pudong attractive in its own right. And it's easy enough to be whisked across the river by taxi, shuttle bus or limousine, or by Metro or ferry, to be back where the action is.

RUIJIN GUEST HOUSE
The accommodation comprises five redbrick villas—mostly dating from the 1920s—in the grounds of what was formerly the Morris Estate. The setting is simply stunning: Within a walled enclosure are a Japanese garden, a small lake and manicured lawns. All rooms are a good size and tastefully decorated and some have balconies overlooking the garden.
➕ E8 ✉ 118 Ruijin Erlu ☎ 6472 5222 🚇 Shaanxi Nanlu

SOFITEL HYLAND SHANGHAI
In a busy part of Nanjing Lu, within an easy walking to the Bund. Business center, fitness center, sauna, delicatessen, bar and several restaurants, including one specializing in Shanghai cooking.
➕ J5 ✉ 505 Nanjing Donglu ☎ 6351 5888
🚇 Nanjing Donglu 🚌 37

TAIYUAN VILLA
This elegant French-Renaissance-style mansion in a secluded garden formerly belonged to US general George Marshall. Most of the accommodations are in villas around the mansion. The Chinese restaurant is the only on-site amenity, but the mansion is near the French Concession.
➕ D8 ✉ 160 Taiyuan Lu ☎ 6471 6688
🚇 Hengshan Lu

Luxury Hotels

GRAND HYATT

www.shanghai.hyatt.com
Spectacular views are the preserve of the Hyatt, which takes the top 34 floors of the Jinmao Tower (▷ 94). All rooms have floor-to-ceiling windows, but those facing the river are the most sought-after.
✚ L7　✉ 88 Shiji Dadao
☎ 5049 1234　🚇 Lujiazui

JIN JIANG TOWER

www.jinjiangtower.com
The more recent version of the old Jin Jiang down the road, the Jin Jiang Tower is a Shanghai landmark in the old French Concession. It contains several restaurants, a business center and a recreation center.
✚ E7　✉ 161 Changle Lu
☎ 6415 1188　🚇 Shaanxi Nanlu　🚌 41

OKURA GARDEN HOTEL SHANGHAI

www.gardennhotelshanghai.com
Close to Huaihai Lu, this hotel has grown up behind the façade of the old French Club. It has three restaurants, including a Japanese one, a business area and a health club.
✚ E7　✉ 58 Maoming Nanlu
☎ 6415 1111　🚇 Shaanxi Nanlu　🚌 41

PORTMAN RITZ CARLTON

www.ritzcarlton.com
This hotel forms part of the Shanghai Center, which is home to shops, restaurants and consulates. The hotel itself has international restaurants, gift shop, health club and business center.
✚ D5　✉ 1376 Nanjing Xilu
☎ 6279 8888　🚇 Jing'an Si　🚌 20, 37

SHANGHAI HILTON

www.hilton.com
With all the hallmarks for which the chain is known, the Hilton is close to the Jing'an Temple and the western part of Nanjing Lu. It has a number of restaurants and a business center.
✚ C6　✉ 250 Huashan Lu
☎ 6248 0000　🚇 Jing'an Si　🚌 45

SHANGHAI JC MANDARIN

www.jcmandarin.com
Offering luxury in the

mold of the famous Hong Kong Mandarin, this hotel has a business center and fitness center, as well as a number of restaurants and pubs.
✚ E5　✉ 1225 Nanjing Xilu
☎ 6279 1888　🚇 Jing'an Si　🚌 20, 37

SHERATON GRAND TAI PING YANG

www.starwoodhotels.com
This comfortable hotel is convenient for the airport, on the western edge of the city. There are six restaurants, a health club and a business center.
✚ Off map　✉ 5 Zunyi Lu
☎ 6275 8888　🚌 57

ST REGIS

www.starwoodhotels.com
Regularly voted one of Asia's best hotels, the St Regis offers the ultimate in luxury and the largest standard rooms in Shanghai. All guests have access to their own butler 24 hours a day.
✚ Off map　✉ 889 Dongfang Lu　☎ 5050 4567
🚇 Dongfang Lu

SUMMIT HUA TING HOTEL & TOWERS

www.summithotels.com
In the southwest of the city close to the Xujiahui Cathedral, Hua Ting is a large, well-established hotel with business and fitness centers, shopping arcade, beauty salon, disco and five restaurants.
✚ Off map　✉ 1200 Caoxi Beilu　☎ 6439 1000
🚇 Shanghai Tiyuyuan
🚌 42, 43, 73

Use this section to help you plan your visit to Shanghai. We have suggested the best ways to get around the city and useful information for when you are there.

Planning Ahead

When to Go

The best time to visit Shanghai is either in the spring (late April/May) or in late summer/early autumn. The days are often clear and warm and therefore comfortable for exploring the city on foot. Spring is the season for fruit blossom, while in the autumn there's Shanghai crab, a specialty of the city.

TIME

Shanghai is 13 hours ahead of New York and 8 hours ahead of the UK. Shanghai does not have daylight saving.

AVERAGE DAILY MAXIMUM TEMPERATURES

JAN	FEB	MAR	APR	MAY	JUN	JUL	AUG	SEP	OCT	NOV	DEC
45°F	46°F	50°F	64°F	73°F	79°F	88°F	86°F	77°F	72°F	61°F	50°F
7°C	8°C	10°C	18°C	23°C	26°C	31°C	30°C	25°C	22°C	16°C	10°C

Spring (March to June) is a pleasant time. The trees begin to blossom in April; May is usually comfortably warm but is often wet.

Summer (June to August) is extremely hot and humid, particularly July and August.

Autumn (September to October) is often pleasantly warm, although September is also one of the wetter months.

Winter (November to February) is fairly cold and dry although it is rare for temperatures to fall below freezing.

WHAT'S ON

The dates of traditional Chinese festivals vary from year to year according to the lunar calendar, which usually begins in February.

Winter/spring *Chinese New Year/Spring Festival*: The most important festival in the Chinese calendar and Christmas and New Year in one, usually falls in February. Red envelopes containing money are given to encourage prosperity. It may be hard to find hotel accommodation at this time and many attractions will be closed.

Lantern Festival (15th day of first lunar month): People walk the streets with illuminated paper lanterns.

Guanyin's Birthday (19th day of the second moon): Guanyin is the goddess of mercy, and on her birthday temples are filled with worshippers.

Longhua Temple Fair (third lunar month): Celebration of the founding of Longhua Temple.

May *International Labour Day* (May 1)

Music Festival: A festival of classical western and traditional music.

June *Children's Day* (Jun 1)

September *Mid-Autumn Festival* (15th day of the eighth moon): Recalls a 14th-century uprising against the Mongols and is now celebrated with Moon cakes, filled with lotus root, dates and sesame.

October *National Day* (Oct 1): Celebration of the founding of the People's Republic of China.

November *Shanghai Marathon*: A major sporting event, when thousands of runners can be seen jostling along Nanjing Lu.

Shanghai Online

http://live.shanghaidaily.com
The English online version of the *Shanghai Daily* presents a somewhat sober style and all the news the government thinks is fit to print. But it contains plenty of useful news, views and information about practical matters.

www.8days.sh
Online general interest magazine about Shanghai, with good entertainment and what's on sections, and decent news coverage.

www.shanghai.gov.cn
The official website of the Shanghai Municipality has an extensive English section covering city news and services, travel, leisure and hotels.

www.shanghaihighlights.com
The Shanghai website of tour operator China Highlights. It features many guided-tour and excursion options in the city.

www.shanghaiist.com
One of the city's best general websites, aimed mainly at the young, footloose, fancy-free and ready-to-party.

www.smartshanghai.com
This hip site aims to get you to the coolest parties, raves, dance clubs and other venues where the action is hot and happening.

www.travelchinaguide.com
This comprehensive general China travel website covers cultural issues in Shanghai in reasonable depth, providing decent introductions to places of interest and practical matters. Note that some information is dated.

www.xianzai.com
Shanghai is just one of several Chinese cities for which this site provides entertainment, dining and travel news and information.

USEFUL TRAVEL SITE

www.fodors.com
A complete travel-planning site. You can research prices and weather; book air tickets, cars and rooms; pose questions to fellow travelers; and find links to other sites.

INTERNET CAFÉS

Amid official unease at the freedom internet cafés afford users to receive information and opinions—and concerns about young people becoming addicted to chatrooms and games—internet cafés face strict controls and are often shut down. The internet is subjected to censorship and controls in China.

Cyber Café
H7 ⊠ 3rd Floor, Hao Du Plaza, 400 Jinling Zhonglu ☎ 6355 7070 ⏱ Daily 1–11 Ⓜ Nanjing Donglu

3 C & T
E7 ⊠ 1st Floor, 238 Shaanxi Nanlu ☎ 6473 0874, ext 229 ⏱ Mon–Fri 10am–2am, Sat–Sun 10–6 Ⓜ Shaanxi Nanlu

Pacific Coffee Company
G5 ⊠ Ground Floor, Hong Kong New World Tower, 300 Huaihai Zhoglu ☎ 6335 3362 ⏱ Daily 7.30–7.30 Ⓜ Huangpi Nanlu

Getting There

AIRPORT TAX

● 50 RMB for domestic flights, 90 RMB for international flights. These taxes are included in the price of air tickets.

ENTRY REQUIREMENTS

● Visitors must hold a valid passport with at least six months' validity.
● Visas for all foreign nationals must be obtained in advance from the nearest Chinese Consulate or Embassy. They are valid for 30 days but can be extended once you arrive in China. Allow five days for its issue. A passport photograph and fee will be required. If in a group you may be visiting on a group visa.
● In Shanghai visa extensions are issued by the Public Security Bureau, ✉ 1500 Minsheng Lu, Pudong.
● No vaccinations are required unless coming from a yellow fever infected area. However, doctors may recommend certain precautionary measures.

AIRPORTS

Shanghai Pudong International Airport (PVG), 19 miles (30km) from the city opened in 1999 and took over all Shanghai's international flights from Hongqiao Airport in 2002. It handles 20 million passengers a year.

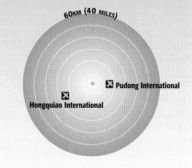

60KM (40 MILES)

☒ Pudong International

☒ Hongqiao International

ARRIVING BY AIR (INTERNATIONAL)

All international, and some domestic, flights arrive at Pudong International Airport (www.shanghaiairport.com). Information counters are by the domestic and international security check areas and airside in the domestic departure area. There is a luggage storage facility in international arrivals (☎ 6834 6078 ⏰ Daily 6am–midnight), and there are shops, restaurants and cafés across the airport. Transportation to Shanghai is by shuttle buses or taxi, or on Maglev, the world's first commercial magnetic levitation rail system. Shuttle buses leave every 10 to 30 minutes from Arrivals; the journey to central Shanghai takes 30–40 minutes (seven routes). Buy tickets on board the bus. Taxi stands are to the right outside the arrivals hall. Have your destination written in Chinese, and ensure the meter is switched on. Ignore the unofficial taxi touts in and just outside the arrivals hall. The trip will take 25–40 minutes, depending on traffic and your destination. Maglev trains traveling at up to 267mph (430kph) take less than 8 minutes to reach Longyang Road Metro station, on Metro line 2. Maglev is accessed via level 2.

ARRIVING BY AIR (DOMESTIC)

For information concerning arriving on domestic flights at Pudong International Airport, ▷ opposite. Some domestic flights arrive at the older and far less-efficient Hongqiao Airport, in the city's western suburbs. Both arrivals halls at Honqiao have hotel shuttle desks, and outside the halls are bus stops for buses to Shanghai Railway Station, Shanghai Stadium, People's Square, Pudong International Airport and other points. Taxis take 30–40 minutes for the trip to the city center.

ARRIVING BY BOAT

Services from Japan are operated by two companies: The Shanghai Ferry Company, a weekly service from Osaka; and the Japan-China International Ferry Co, a weekly service from Kobe. Crossings take two days; ships dock at the International Passenger Terminal in Hongkou.

Most passengers arriving in Shanghai by boat do so on ferries from ports on the East China Sea (Ningbo) and the Yangtze River (Wuhan, Chongqing). These dock at the Wusong Passenger Terminal in the north of the city.

ARRIVING BY TRAIN

Shanghai's main station is in the north of the city on Jiaotong Lu. Taxis are readily available at the station to take you onward, and the Shanghai Huochezhan Metro station is close by. Remember to retain your ticket until you are out of the terminal. The station itself is large, busy and complicated. It is invariably surrounded by large crowds of people looking for or waiting for work, and by individuals who hope to hustle arriving foreigners. It makes sense to be sure that you are not overburdened with luggage and can make your way quickly and smoothly to the taxi stands outside (ignoring touts who offer you a taxi on the way). Getting to the Metro station with a lot of luggage, or with small children in tow, is sure to be far more stressful than waiting for a taxi.

CUSTOMS REGULATIONS

● You may import 400 cigarettes, 2 litres of alcohol, 0.5 litres of perfume.
● When departing be careful that any antique you have purchased is permitted to leave the country. Antiques that are permitted for export must bear a red seal and any item not carrying the seal may be seized at customs.

VISITORS WITH A DISABILITY

China is not a country that has made many concessions to people with disabilities. However, very slowly, things are improving. As new hotels and museums are constructed, so access is being made easier for wheelchair users and wheelchairs are more readily available at airports. However, attitudes, in general, are not thoughtful or considerate—you should be prepared for difficulties and for the need to improvise.

INSURANCE

● Travel insurance covering medical expenses is essential.
● In the event of medical treatment, be sure to keep all receipts.

Getting Around

MAPS

Basic tourist maps of Shanghai are widely available from bookshops, hotels and CITS.

WALKING BLUES

While getting around on foot is a great way to see the city, remember that distances are large and the streets are filled with pedestrians, traffic and noise. It can be exhausting, particularly in summer. It makes more sense to go by taxi or public transportation to the general area you want to explore and walk from there. Be cautious at all times when crossing roads, even at traffic lights. Shanghai's drivers show no mercy to mere pedestrians.

TAXI TRIALS

It's asking for trouble to step into one of the illegal taxis that operate from the airports, rail stations and other locations around town. You are certain to be vastly overcharged and can face aggression if you try to resist paying.

BICYCLES

● Bicycles (*zixingche*) are widely used and can be rented at little cost from some hotels or from specialist outlets.

● Check brakes and tires before setting out and observe how traffic functions in China—joining it unprepared can be an unnerving experience.

BUSES

● The comprehensive bus system is very inexpensive but the buses can be extremely crowded, especially close to the rush hour.

● Buses run between 5am and 11pm.

● The best tourist bus routes are: the No. 11, which shuttles around the Old Town; the No. 16, which runs between the banks of the Huangpu and the Old Town and the Jade Buddha Temple; the No. 18, which runs between the railway station, Xizang Lu and the river; and the No. 65, which runs between the Bund and close to the railway station.

● Make sure that you have small change—you pay your fare on board.

● Note that pushing one's way on board is a feature of daily life. Pickpockets are not unknown.

FERRIES

● Ferries cross the Huangpu River between Pudong and the Bund from 6am to 11.30pm.

● Return fares are 2–4RMB.

METRO

● The opening of the still-unfinished Line 4 in early 2006 took the number of lines to five, covering a distance of 123km (77 miles). By 2009, another six lines and more than 100 new stations will have been added, with further extensions to existing lines.

● The busiest station is People's Square, intersected by Lines 1 and 2. Line 1 runs from Gonfu Xincun in the north to Xinzhuang, via Shanghai railway station. Line 2 goes east from Zhongshan Park and links to the Maglev at Longyang Road, crossing under the Huangpu

River. Lujiazui station serves the Oriental Pearl Tower in the Pudong financial district, opposite the Bund waterfront. Line 3 runs south from Jiangwan Zhen, looping west alongside Line 4 via Shanghai rail station. Line 5 extends west and south from Line 1's southerly terminus, Xinhuang.

● Trains run every few minutes from 5.30 or 6 in the morning until 10.30 or 11 in the evening, and platform screens show the next two trains due. Signs and announcements are in English and Chinese.

● Fares range from 2RMB to 8RMB. Travel in the central area on Lines 1 and 2 costs 3–4RMB. SIngle tickets can be bought from station concourse vending machines or at ticket windows. For multiple journeys, buy a Shanghai Public Transportation Card, an electronic smart card swiped on automated ticket barriers. Refundable cards costing 30RMB are available from stations and convenience stores and can be topped up as desired. The cards can also be used for buses, taxis and ferries.

● Overcrowding is a problem during rush hours, notably at People's Square. Glass safety screens with sliding doors have been installed on some platform edges.

● Shanghai Metro lines are being renamed. Each line number will be prefixed by a letter identifying it as an elevated light railway (L), a central business district subway (M) or one serving the suburbs (R).

TAXIS

● Taxis are widely available, metered and easy to flag down.

● Travel by taxi is quite inexpensive and definitely the best way of getting around, occasional traffic jams notwithstanding.

● In general, Shanghai taxi drivers are very honest. However, if you are dissatisfied, take note of the licence number displayed inside.

● Never accept an offer from someone who approaches you for a taxi. There are plenty of legal taxis.

RETURN ADDRESS

Always carry with you a card or handwritten note in Chinese stating your hotel name and address, and perhaps even directions for how to get there if it is not likely to be well known or in an easily identifiable location. This will be particularly useful for taxi drivers—but might also come in handy should you be involved in an accident or lose your wallet or handbag. An extension of this precaution would be to carry information in Chinese about any chronic medical condition you have or medicines you need to take.

SIDE TRIPS

Shanghai is within striking distance of several of China's most interesting small—by Chinese standards—cities: Suzhou (the city of classic Chinese gardens); Hangzhou (described by Marco Polo as paradise on earth, and noted for its beautiful West Lake, Xihu); Nanjing (a former capital on the Yangtze, with historical tombs and other sights on forested hills above the river); and Wuxi (the most convenient gateway to Lake Tai/Taihu). All of these can be reached by organized tour, or by train from Shanghai. Have someone at your hotel write down your destination in Chinese.

Essential Facts

EMERGENCY NUMBERS

● Ambulance ☎ 120
● Fire ☎ 119
● Police ☎ 110

MONEY

RMB (Renminbi) is the currency of China. The basic unit is the yuan (pronounced "kuai"), made up of 10 jiao (pronounced "mao"), each of which is again divided into 10 fen. There are notes for 1, 2, 5, 10, 20, 50 and 100 yuan, and the smaller 1, 2 and 5 jiao. There are also coins for 1, 2 and 5 yuan; 1, 2 and 5 jiao; and 1, 2 and 5 fen.

20 yuan

50 yuan

100 yuan

ELECTRICITY

● The power supply is 220V, 50 cycles AC.
● Plugs types vary, the most common is the two-flat-pin type. It is worth taking an adaptor.

ETIQUETTE

● Avoid displays of anger and aggression. If you have a complaint, gentle, persistent questioning is the best way of dealing with it.
● Remember that China is a totalitarian country where unorthodox opinions are discouraged.
● The language barrier means that irony is wasted and you may be placed in the embarrassing position of having to explain what was intended merely as a wry observation.
● Though table etiquette continues to be observed at banquets, generally table manners are nonexistent. Spitting and hawking are widespread and cigarette smoking common.

MEDICAL TREATMENT

● Treatment is available in state hospitals and in private, joint-venture clinics.
● For minor ailments the foreigner section of the state-run hospitals will normally be the cheapest option. However, try to ascertain the cost of treatment in advance.
● Your host organization (eg. CITS) or hotel will help to put you in contact with a hospital.
● Private clinics: New Pioneer Medical Centre ✉ 910 Hengshan Lu ☎ 6469 3898; World Link Medical Centre ✉ Shanghai Center, 1376 Nanjing Xilu ☎ 6445 5999; Sino-Canadian Dental Center ✉ Ninth People's Hospital, 639 Zhizao Julu ☎ 6313 31741 ext. 5276; Shanghai Ko Sei Dental Clinic ✉ 666 Changle Lu ☎ 6247 7000.
● State hospitals: Hua Dong Hospital, Foreigners' Clinic ✉ 221 Yan'an Xilu ☎ 6248 3180 ext. 3106; Huashan Hospital, Foreigners' Clinic ✉ 12 Wulumuqi Zhonglu ☎ 6248 3986; IMCC in First People's Hospital ✉ 585 Jiulong ☎ 66306 9480; Pediatric Hospital, Foreigners' Clinic ✉ Medical Center of Fudan University, 183 Fenglin Lu ☎ 6404 1990.

MEDICINES
● Western medicines are available but can be expensive. Traditional Chinese medicine is effective but is often a slow process.
● If you have particular medical needs, make sure that you are equipped to satisfy them before you visit China.

MONEY MATTERS
● Money can be changed in most hotels. A passport may be required.
● Credit cards are accepted in international hotels and shops but not in small shops.
● RMB can be changed back into foreign currency when leaving China but you must produce relevant exchange receipts.

POST OFFICES
● The main post office is on the corner of Suzhou Beilu and Sichuan Beilu.
● Stamps can be purchased from most hotels.
● Post boxes are normally green; but you can hand your mail to the hotel receptionist.

TELEPHONES
● Local calls can be made from public phone boxes (coins or cards) all over the city.
● Long-distance calls can be made from call boxes but not usually international calls.
● Local calls from hotel rooms are often free. International direct dialing is expensive.
● The international access code from China is 00. Or call 108 to get through to a local operator in the country being called, through whom a reverse charge call can be made.

TIPPING
● Despite official disapproval, tipping is no longer an offense; indeed it is now expected by tourist guides who prefer money—US dollars are popular—to a gift. Hotel porters will usually happily accept a tip, and so will taxi drivers although it is not necessarily expected. In most restaurants, tips are not usually expected, except in some of the top establishments.

TOILETS
● Western-style toilets are common in hotels and in many restaurants but the traditional hole in the ground is also widely used.
● Public toilets are not generally available and those that do exist can be distinctly unsanitary. More and better facilities are gradually appearing but you are advised to carry your own paper and soap.

TOURIST OFFICES
● Shanghai does not have tourist information offices. Most people still travel in groups so the main source of information will be from local guides; individual visitors have to rely on their own ingenuity. The China International Travel Service (CITS, the state-run travel service) is becoming more professional in its outlook and will often help even when you are not organizing your trip through them, otherwise, try an independent agent.
● China International Travel Service: ✉ 8th floor No. 1277 Beijing Lu ☎ 6321 7200
● Tourist hotline ☎ 6439 8947

Language

The official language of China is known as Mandarin in the West, or *putonghua* in China, and is based on the dialect of Beijing. It is spoken throughout China but local dialects are commonly used—the Shanghai dialect is quite different from *putonghua*. However, knowledge of a few *putonghua* words and phrases will undoubtedly be an advantage at some point.

USEFUL WORDS AND PHRASES

GREETINGS

hello/how are you	*ni hao*
please	*qing*
thank you	*xiexie*
good-bye	*zai jian*
cheers!	*gan bei*
no problem	*mei wen ti*
I'm fine	*wo hen hao*
My surname is…	*wo xing…*
I am from…	*who shi laide…*

IN THE HOTEL

hotel	*binguan, fandian*
room	*fang jian*
bathroom	*xishu jian*

POST OFFICES, BANKS AND SHOPS

post office	*youju*
stamp	*you piao*
postcard	*ming xin pian*
airmail	*hang kong*
letter	*xin*
telephone	*dianhua*
bank	*yin hang*
money exchange	*huan qian chu*

how much?	*Duo shao qian?*
too expensive	*tai gui le*
a little cheaper	*pian yi dian ba*
gift	*li wu*
credit card	*xin yong ka*
antique	*guwu*
silk	*sichou*
jade	*yu*
carpet	*di tan*
rice	*mifan*
beer	*pijiu*
coffee	*ka fei*

EATING OUT

restaurant	*fan guan, fan dian, can ting*
do you have a menu in English?	*you mei you ying wen cai dan?*
water/cooled	*shui/liang*
boiled water	*kaishui*
coffee	*kafei*
black tea	*hong cha*
beer	*pi jiu*
soft drink	*qi shui*
rice	*mi fan*
fork	*cha zi*

GETTING AROUND

bus	*gong gong qi che*
bus station	*qi che zhan*
boat	*chuan*
bicycle	*zixing che*
taxi	*chu zu qi che*
train	*huo che*
toilet	*cesuo*

HEALTH

I feel ill	*wo bu shu fu*
I would like	*wo xiang*
doctor	*yi sheng*
Aspirin	*zhitongpian*
hospital	*yiyuan*
pharmacy	*yaodian*

COLORS

black	*hei se*
brown	*he se*
pink	*fen hong se*
red	*hong se*
orange	*ju se*
yellow	*huang se*
green	*lu se*
blue	*lan se*
purple	*zi se*
white	*bai se*
gold	*jin se*
silver	*yin se*
gray	*hui se*
turquoise	*qian lan se*

DAYS/MONTHS

Monday	Xing qi yi	March	san yue
Tuesday	Xing qi er	April	si yue
Wednesday	Xing qi san	May	wu yue
Thursday	Xing qi si	June	liu yue
Friday	Xing qi wu	July	qi yue
Saturday	Xing qi liu	August	ba yue
Sunday	Xing qi	September	jiu yue
		October	shi yue
January	yi yue	November	shi yi yue
February	er yue	December	shi er yue

USEFUL WORDS

yes	shi	why	wei shen me
no	bu	who	shei
you're welcome	bu ke qi	may I/can I	Wo ke yi/wo neng
excuse me!	dui bu qi	open	kai
where	zai na li	closed	guan bi
here	zher	church	jiao tang
there	nar	museum	bo wu guan
when	shen me shi hou	monument	ji nian bei
		palace	gong dian

NUMBERS

0	ling	16	shi liu
1	yi	17	shi qi
2	er	18	shi ba
3	san	19	shi jiu
4	si	20	er shi
5	wu	21	er shi yi
6	liu	30	san shi
7	qi	40	si shi
8	ba	50	wu shi
9	jiu	60	liu shi
10	shi	70	qi shi
11	shi yi	80	ba shi
12	shi er	90	jiu shi
13	shi san	100	yi bai
14	shi si	1,000	yi qian
15	shi wu	million	bai wan

PRONUNCIATION

The modern phonetic romanized form of Chinese is called "pinyin". It is largely pronounced as written, but note the following:

a as in car

c as in bits when an initial consonant

e as in her

i as in feet unless preceded by c, ch, r, s, sh, z, zh, when it becomes er as in her

j as in gin

o as in ford

q like the ch in chin

s as in simple

u as in oo in cool

w as in wade, though pronounced by some as v

x like the sh in sheep but with the s given greater emphasis

y as in yoyo

z as ds in lids; zh as j in jam

ENGLISH

English is widely spoken in hotels and in places where foreigners congregate. In general, however, you will find that little English is spoken. A major exception is young people, who learn English at school; many of them speak at least a moderate amount of English and a growing number of young professionals are fluent.

Timeline

THE GANGSTERS

Prewar Shanghai was an iniquitous place, fully deserving of its soubriquet as the "whore of the Orient." Nothing illustrates this better than the roles played by the gangsters, Pockmarked Huang (Huang Jinrong) and Big-eared Du (Du Yuesheng), who ran protection rackets, organized drug smuggling and controlled the city's many prostitutes. Du would warn the targets of his protection rackets of the dangers of Shanghai life by delivering a coffin to their door; Huang enjoyed perfect immunity— he was also Chief Detective for the French Sûreté.

Below left to right: Exterior of the Museum of the First Chinese Communist Party Congress; a display in the Shanghai Museum of Chinese History; a bust of Soong Qing-Ling; Mao and revolutionaries on badges at Dongtai Antiques Market; detail of a bronze plaque, celebrating the Communist liberation of the city, at the Customs House on the Bund

1300s The trading center of Shanghai becomes a county seat under the jurisdiction of Jiangsu Province.

1553 The people of Shanghai build a city wall during the Ming dynasty (1368–1644) to protect them from Japanese pirates.

1842 The Opium Wars reach Shanghai, which is sacked by the British. The Treaty of Nanking, signed in August, permits them to undertake unlimited trade (Concessions), in Shanghai and four other coastal cities.

1863 The British and American Concessions merge to form the International Settlement, while the French Concession remains autonomous. The foreign community enjoys "extraterritoriality," which places it outside Chinese law.

1911 The Qing dynasty falls and China becomes a republic. In 1912, the city walls are demolished to create more space.

1917 Refugees from the Russian Revolution bring a new style to Shanghai entertainment— with outrageous cabarets. Shanghai emerges as the "whore of the Orient."

1927 Chiang Kai Shek is permitted by the foreign community to move troops against the Communists through the Concessions. On 12 April, the Nationalists attack the Communists in Zhabei, killing 20 and arresting several hundred, including Zhou En Lai.

1930s Japan occupies Shanghai and remains in power until the end of World War II.

1949 Mao becomes leader of China and Communist troops enter Shanghai. Few foreigners remain. This is the beginning of the end for the Shanghai of excess.

1966 The beginning of the Cultural Revolution, a period of brutality and terror. Shanghai, China's most industrialized and politically radical city, is the first to enter the fray. Violent rebel groups roam the streets.

1972 The Shanghai Communiqué is signed between China and the US in the Jinjiang Hotel, signifying the end of China's isolation from the outside world.

1976 Mao dies. The Gang of Four, including Mao's widow, make the city their base in their attempt to seize power.

1990s Shanghai re-enters the industrial world, becoming an autonomous municipality running its own affairs. Pudong is declared a Special Economic Zone, where free trade is allowed.

2007 Work begins on the new Shanghai–Beijing high-speed rail line and on a new high-speed Maglev line between Shanghai and Hangzhou (a Maglev train with a top speed of 267mph/430kph between Pudong Airport and the city center has been operating since 2003).

THE GANG OF FOUR

All four members of the so-called Gang of Four, who tried to seize power following the death of Chairman Mao, had Shanghai connections. Jiang Qing, Mao's last wife, was a Shanghai actress. Chang Chun Qiao had been a journalist and director of propaganda in Shanghai. Yao Wen Yuan had been editor of the newspaper *Shanghai Liberation Army Daily*. Wang Hong Wen had been a Shanghai worker and founder member of the Shanghai Workers Revolutionary Headquarters.

WORLD EXPO

In 2002, Shanghai won the competition to host the World Expo in 2010, and it is preparing for its moment in the international spotlight with every bit as much gusto—and with a lot less posturing—as Beijing displayed in getting ready to host the 2008 Olympics.

NEED TO KNOW TIMELINE

Index

CITYPACK TOP 25
Shanghai

WRITTEN BY Christopher Knowles
ADDITIONAL WRITING George McDonald
DESIGN CONCEPT Kate Harling
COVER DESIGN AND DESIGN WORK Jacqueline Bailey
INDEXER Marie Lorimer
IMAGE RETOUCHING AND REPRO Michael Moody, Sarah Montgomery and Matt Swann
EDITOR Bookwork Creative Associates Ltd
SERIES EDITOR Paul Mitchell

© **AUTOMOBILE ASSOCIATION DEVELOPMENTS LIMITED 2008**

First published 1999
New edition 2007
Reprinted June 2008
Colour separation by Keenes
Printed and bound by Leo, China

A CIP catalogue record for this book is available from the British Library.

ISBN 978-0-7495-5495-8

Published by AA Publishing, a trading name of Automobile Association Developments Limited, whose registered office is Fanum House, Basing View, Basingstoke, Hampshire RG21 4EA. Registered number 1878835.

A03839
Maps in this title produced from mapping © MAIRDUMONT / Falk Verlag 2008
Transport map © Communicarta Ltd, UK

The Automobile Association would like to thank the following photographers, companies and picture libraries for their assistance in the preparation of this book.

Abbreviations for the picture credits are as follows – (t) top; (b) bottom; (c) centre; (l) left; (r) right; (AA) AA World Travel Library.

F/C AA/A Mockford & N Bonetti; **B/C(t)** AA/A Mockford & N Bonetti; **B/C(tc)** AA/C Sawyer; **B/C(bc)** AA/A Mockford & N Bonetti; **B/C(b)** AA/G D R Clements; **1** AA/A Mockford & N Bonetti; **2/3t** AA/G D R Clements; **4/5t** AA/G D R Clements; **4t** AA/G D R Clements; **5** AA/I Morejohn; **6/7t** AA/G D R Clements; **6cl** AA/A Mockford & N Bonetti; **6cc** AA/G D R Clements; **6cr** AA/D Henley; **6bl** AA/A Mockford & N Bonetti; **6bc** AA/A Mockford & N Bonetti; **6br** AA/A Mockford & N Bonetti; **7cl** AA/ G D R Clements; **7ccl** AA/G D R Clements; **7ccr** AA/G D R Clements; **7cr** AA/G D R Clements; **7bl** AA/G D R Clements; **7bc** AA/A Mockford & N Bonetti; **7br** AA/G D R Clements; **8/9t** AA/I AA/ AA/G D R Clements; **10t** AA/G D R Clements; **10b** AA/G D R Clements; **10/1c** AA/G D R Clements; **10/1b** AA/G D R Clements; **11t** AA/A Mockford & N Bonetti; **11b** AA/G D R Clements; **12/3t** AA/G D R Clements; **13t** AA/A Mockford & N Bonetti; **13ct** AA/A Mockford & N Bonetti; **13c** AA/A Kouprianoff; **13bc** AA/A Mockford & N Bonetti; **13b** AA/G D R Clements; **14/5t** AA/G D R Clements; **14t** AA/A Mockford & N Bonetti; **14tc** AA/ A Mockford & N Bonetti; **14bc** AA/A Kouprianoff; **14b** AA/A Mockford & N Bonetti; **15** AA/G D R Clements; **16/7t** AA/G D R Clements; **16t** AA/A Mockford & N Bonetti; **16tc** AA/A Mockford & N Bonetti; **16bc** AA/A Mockford & N Bonetti; **16b** AA/D Henley; **17t** AA/ G D R Clements; **17c** AA/A Mockford & N Bonetti; **17b** ©Robin Whalley/Alamy; **18t** AA/G D R Clements; **18tc** AA/G D R Clements; **18c** AA/A Mockford & N Bonetti; **18cb** AA/A Mockford & N Bonetti; **18b** AA/A Mockford & N Bonetti; **19(I)** AA/ G D R Clements; **19(II)** AA/ A Mockford & N Bonetti; **19(III)** AA/A Mockford & N Bonetti; **19(IV)** AA/G D R Clements; **19(V)** AA/G D R Clements; **19(VI)** AA/A Mockford & N Bonetti; **19(VII)** AA/ G D R Clements; **20/1** AA/G D R Clements; **24l** AA/A Mockford & N Bonetti; **24tr** AA/A Mockford & N Bonetti; **24br** AA/A Mockford & N Bonetti; **25t** AA/A Mockford & N Bonetti; **25bl** AA/A Mockford & N Bonetti; **25br** AA/A Mockford & N Bonetti; **26l** AA/ G D R Clements; **26c** AA/G D R Clements; **26r** AA/G D R Clements; **27l** AA/G D R Clements; **27r** AA/G D R Clements; **28l** AA/A Mockford & N Bonetti; **28r** AA/A Kouprianoff; **29l** AA/G D R Clements; **29r** AA/G D R Clements; **30t** AA/A Mockford & N Bonetti; **30bl** AA/G D R Clements; **30br** AA/A Mockford & N Bonetti; **31t** AA/G D R Clements; **31b** AA/A Mockford & N Bonetti; **32** AA/A Mockford & N Bonetti; **33** AA/A Mockford & N Bonetti; **36l** AA/I Morejohn; **36r** AA/A Kouprianoff; **37l** AA/A Mockford & N Bonetti; **37r** AA/A Mockford & N Bonetti; **38l** AA/A Mockford & N Bonetti; **38/9** ©Kevin Foy/Alamy; **39t** ©Tibor Bognar/Alamy; **39bl** ©Kevin Foy/Alamy; **39br** AA/G D R Clements; **40l** AA/A Mockford & N Bonetti; **40r** AA/A Mockford & N Bonetti; **41l** AA/A Mockford & N Bonetti; **41r** ©Kevin Foy/Alamy; **42l** AA/G D R Clements; **42tr** AA/A Mockford & N Bonetti; **42br** AA/G D R Clements; **43t** AA/ G D R Clements; **43bl** AA/A Mockford & N Bonetti; **43br** AA/A Mockford & N Bonetti; **44l** AA/A Mockford & N Bonetti; **44r** AA/A Mockford & N Bonetti; **45t** AA/A Mockford & N Bonetti; **45bl** AA/A Mockford & N Bonetti; **45br** AA/G D R Clements; **46** AA/A Mockford & N Bonetti; **47** AA/A Mockford & N Bonetti; **48/9** AA/I Morejohn; **50** AA/A Kouprianoff; **51** AA/A Kouprianoff; **52** AA/A Mockford & N Bonetti; **53** AA/A Mockford & N Bonetti; **56l** ©Robert Harding Picture Library Ltd/ Alamy; **56r** ©Paul Harris/Onasia.com; **57t** AA/G D R Clements; **57bl** ©Jesper Haynes/Onasia.com; **57br** ©Paul Harris/Onasia.com; **58l** AA/A Mockford & N Bonetti; **58tr** AA/A Mockford & N Bonetti; **58/9b** AA/A Mockford & N Bonetti; **59t** AA/A Mockford & N Bonetti; **59bl** AA/A Mockford & N Bonetti; **59br** AA/A Mockford & N Bonetti; **60** AA/A Mockford & N Bonetti; **61t** AA/A Mockford & N Bonetti; **61b** ©LOOK Die Bildagentur der Fotografen GmbH/Alamy; **62l** AA/A Mockford & N Bonetti; **62r** AA/ G D R Clements; **63t** Gavin Hellier/Robert Harding; **63bl** Gavin Hellier/Robert Harding; **63br** AA/A Mockford & N Bonetti; **64** AA/A Mockford & N Bonetti; **65t** AA/G D R Clements; **65b** AA/G D R Clements; **66** AA/A Mockford & N Bonetti; **67** AA/A Mockford & N Bonetti; **70t** AA/G D R Clements; **70b** AA/G D R Clements; **70/1t** AA/G D R Clements; **70/1b** AA/G D R Clements; **71t** AA/G D R Clements; **71b** AA/G D R Clements; **72tl** AA/A Mockford & N Bonetti; **72bl** AA/A Mockford & N Bonetti; **72tr** AA/A Mockford & N Bonetti; **72br** AA/G D R Clements; **73t** AA/G D R Clements; **73bl** AA/G D R Clements; **73br** AA/A Mockford & N Bonetti; **74l** AA/G D R Clements; **74r** AA/G D R Clements; **75t** AA/A Mockford & N Bonetti; **75bl** AA/ A Mockford & N Bonetti; **75br** AA/A Mockford & N Bonetti; **76t** AA/A Mockford & N Bonetti; **76bl** AA/ A Mockford & N Bonetti; **76br** AA/A Mockford & N Bonetti; **77** AA/ A Mockford & N Bonetti; **78t** AA/G D R Clements; **79t** AA/A Mockford & N Bonetti; **80** AA/A Mockford & N Bonetti; **81** AA/G D R Clements; **84l** AA/A Mockford & N Bonetti; **84r** AA/A Mockford & N Bonetti; **85** AA/A Mockford & N Bonetti; **86l** AA/G D R Clements; **86r** AA/G D R Clements; **87t** AA/A Mockford & N Bonetti; **87b** AA/G D R Clements; **88** AA/A Mockford & N Bonetti; **89** AA/A Mockford & N Bonetti; **92t** AA/G D R Clements; **92bl** AA/A Mockford & N Bonetti; **92br** AA/G D R Clements; **93l** AA/G D R Clements; **93r** AA/A Mockford & N Bonetti; **94** AA/A Mockford & N Bonetti; **94/5** AA/A Mockford & N Bonetti; **95** AA/A Mockford & N Bonetti; **96t** AA/A Mockford & N Bonetti; **96b** AA/A Mockford & N Bonetti; **97t** AA/G D R Clements; **97b** AA/A Mockford & N Bonetti; **98** AA/A Mockford & N Bonetti; **99** AA/G D R Clements; **102tl** AA/A Kouprianoff; **102tr** AA/A Kouprianoff; **102bl** AA/G D R Clements; **102br** AA/G D R Clements; **103t** AA/G D R Clements; **103b** AA/A Kouprianoff; **104l** AA/G D R Clements; **104r** AA/G D R Clements; **105** AA/G D R Clements; **106** Corbis; **107** AA/A Mockford & N Bonetti; **108/9t** AA/C Sawyer; **108/9b** AA/A Mockford & N Bonetti; **108tcr** AA; **108cbr** AA/G D R Clements; **108br** AA/G D R Clements; **110/1** AA/C Sawyer; **112** AA/C Sawyer; **113** AA/A Mockford & N Bonetti; **114/5** AA/A Mockford & N Bonetti; **116/7t** AA/A Mockford & N Bonetti; **118/9t** AA/A Mockford & N Bonetti; **120/1t** AA/A Mockford & N Bonetti; **122/3t** AA/A Mockford & N Bonetti; **124/5t** AA/A Mockford & N Bonetti; **124bl** AA/A Mockford & N Bonetti; **124br** AA/G D R Clements; **125bl** AA/G D R Clements; **125bc** AA/A Mockford & N Bonetti; **125br** AA/A Mockford & N Bonetti.

Every effort has been made to trace the copyright holders, and we apologise in advance for any accidental errors. We would be happy to apply the corrections in the following edition of this publication.